Editor
Lorin E. Klistoff, M.A.

Managing Editor
Karen Goldfluss, M.S. Ed.

Editor-in-Chief
Sharon Coan, M.S. Ed.

Illustrator
Kevin Barnes
Howard Chaney

Cover Artist
Barb Lorseyedi

Art Coordinator
Kevin Barnes

Art Director
CJae Froshay

Imaging
James Edward Grace

Product Manager
Phil Garcia

Publishers
Rachelle Cracchiolo, M.S. Ed.
Mary Dupuy Smith, M.S. Ed.

Creative Classroom IDEAS

Ways to Motivate, Manage, and Spice Up Your Daily Routine

Author

Michelle Scavo Bonus

Teacher Created Materials, Inc.
6421 Industry Way
Westminster, CA 92683
www.teachercreated.com

ISBN 0-7439-3655-8

©2002 Teacher Created Materials, Inc.
Made in U.S.A.

Table of Contents

Introduction

Looking for innovative ideas to easily incorporate into your already existing classroom? Or maybe you are a first-time teacher needing proven, effective, simple, and unique activities to use in your new classroom. In either case, you have found the right book!

Creative Classroom Ideas has been designed for any teacher, kindergarten through eighth grade, who is looking for activities that are general enough to use any time, for any age group, and any ability level. The ideas have been proven to be effective in any classroom! You will also find the activities require little preparation and can be incorporated with ease.

This book appeals to both veteran and beginning teachers. Veteran teachers will find new activities to introduce, as well as spice up, their daily routine and instruction that is already in place. A beginning teacher will find the ideas of particular interest, because they provide easy and fun activities to use along with the enormous amount of new curriculum they will be required to teach. Because of its broad range, all teachers will find the book to be useful!

Motivational Ideas

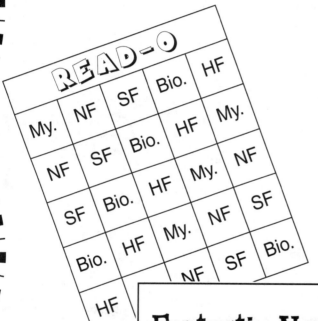

READ-O

My.	NF	SF	Bio.	HF
NF	SF	Bio.	HF	My.
SF	Bio.	HF	My.	NF
Bio.	HF	My.	NF	SF
HF		NF	SF	Bio.

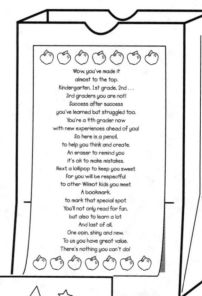

Wow, you've made it
almost to the top.
Kindergarten, 1st grade, 2nd . . .
3rd graders you are not!
Success after success
you've learned but struggled too.
You're a 4th grader now
with new experiences ahead of you!
So here is a pencil,
to help you think and create.
An eraser to remind you
it's ok to make mistakes.
Next a lollipop to keep you sweet
for you will be respectful
to other Wilmot kids you meet.
A bookmark,
to mark that special spot.
You'll not only read for fun,
but also to learn a lot.
And last of all,
One coin, shiny and new.
To us you have great value.
There's nothing you can't do!

Fantastic News!

This is to report that

_____

has

_____

_____

Congratulations!

Participation Ante

Are students not participating enough? Are the same students always participating while others just sit? Try a tally device to make the teacher and students aware of how often they are participating in whole-class activities and/or discussions.

For each activity, place three of anything on each student's desk—right in front for easy access and visibility. Sticky notes are good, because they aren't interesting enough for students to want to play with them, they stay in one place, and they don't end up on the floor. Every time a child participates in the activity, take one sticky note off his or her desk. Students left with sticky notes are quickly aware of how little they are involved.

A fun way of introducing the activity is to put the notes on each desk, but do not tell students what they are for. Just say you will be removing them, and that it is a good thing to have them removed. It is up to them to figure out why they are being removed. Students will soon figure it out. Once they understand the concept, the teacher can start over with another subject area.

This is a really helpful way for a teacher to pinpoint those students who avoid participation. The teacher will also be able to see a pattern—one student may always participate in reading, but rarely during math. This can be valuable information.

Squiggle Stories

Ideas to Stimulate Writers

Are students running out of ideas to write creative stories? Squiggle pictures give students just enough motivation to get them excited about writing again. Follow the instructions below.

1. On large pieces of white construction paper, use a thick marker to draw a random squiggle on each piece. Make each squiggle out of the same color marker so it is identifiable on each piece.

2. Give each student a paper. Then each student turns his or her paper as needed until he or she can see a shape or object come through.

3. Each student then adds to the squiggle to form the picture he or she sees.

4. After the picture is complete, each student writes a story about the picture. Or, he or she can incorporate the picture in some part of his or her story. Maybe the squiggle picture is a sailboat, so the story can be about an exploring adventure on this man-made sailboat.

5. Display pictures with the story so other students can read and enjoy!

✓ **Tip:** Instead of creating an object, have the students create a newly discovered animal or insect out of the squiggle. (See sample on page 7.) Once they have drawn this new creature or species, they can write an expository paper about the creature. The teacher can make up a pretend class encyclopedia where these entries will go. These creative papers will now turn into a report which tells the habitat of the creature, what it eats, looks like, how it catches its food, etc. It is a way to practice a formal writing style while using creativity too!

Ideas to Stimulate Artists

Want to stimulate some artists? How about getting students to pay attention to detail? Have them illustrate a chapter of a book the teacher reads aloud to the class. Follow the instructions below.

1. The teacher can pick two students to sit in the back of the room away from each other.

2. As the teacher reads the chapter aloud, they draw a picture of an interesting event.

3. At the end of the chapter, illustrators share the drawings with the class.

4. Each day the teacher picks two new students to illustrate what has been read.

5. After the story is complete, the teacher can compile all the drawings in a class book. If desired, let students sign their artwork.

✓ **Tips:** Variations include having the whole class illustrate at the same time. Small groups can also be formed with one member of each group illustrating a chapter a day. Then the small group can share their completed book of drawings when the whole story is finished. For variation, students can paint with watercolors rather than draw.

Squiggle Story Sample Drawing

"The Geed Bird"

The Geed Bird is a very tall and unusual creature. The Geed Bird has enormous eyes and extremely good distance vision. The legs are skinny and hold most of the weight of the bird. The Geed Bird lives mostly in warm climates and loves to eat large insects, such as crickets.

Individual Mini Conferences

It never fails, once that report card comes out there are always those few students who question the marks they receive in one area or another. Inevitably, if a student has a question, parents will too. A great way to avoid any surprises is to hold individual conferences with students at least twice a year. If the teacher can, every quarter would be ideal. These mini conferences give the teacher a chance to praise each student and let them know the areas the teacher feels they need help with. In addition, it is a wonderful time for students to tell the teacher how they are feeling about school, friends, or whatever is on their mind. Mini conferences stop problems in all areas before they get too large.

Students like to have one-on-one time with their teacher. They also like to feel they are heard and understood. Mini conferences really help establish a strong relationship between the teacher and student.

Pick a time of day when students are independently working or reading. Have a notebook in hand to make notes or use the Mini Conference Sheet located on page 9. If a child mentions a particular concern, jot it down for future reference. It is also wise to write down what the teacher mentioned to the child so the teacher can have a reminder of what was discussed.

When report cards are given out, the mini conference should help clarify any questions the student has about the report card, keeping surprises minimal. Since the teacher has met with each student, students can now explain to their parents any questions they have about the report card as well. It is also a good thing for the teacher to let the parents know that he or she has spoken to their child already about a particular issue that may appear on the report card.

Mini Conference Sheet

Name _____ Date _____

Questions

1. Do you have any friendship concerns?

   _____

   _____

2. Do you have any academic concerns (any particular difficulties in a certain area)?

   _____

   _____

3. How is the homework for you?

   _____

4. What is your favorite part of school?

   _____

   _____

   _____

5. What is your least favorite part of school?

   _____

   _____

   _____

Specific Student Goals

_____

_____

_____

Notes

_____

_____

_____

_____

READ-O

A fun way to encourage students to read various genres of books is to play READ-O. READ-O is similar to Bingo in that each child has a game board and needs to get five in a row to win. (See page 11 for READ-O Game Board.) The squares on the READ-O board represent different genres: mystery, nonfiction, science fiction, biography, and historical fiction. When a student finishes reading one of the READ-O genres, he or she fills out the book log (page 12 or 13) and conferences with the teacher about the book. The conference is a brief discussion about the book to ensure the student understood what was read. After the conference, the student can put a sticker or a stamp on one of the squares of the game board that corresponds to the genre he or she has completed. Once five stickers in a row have been placed on the READ-O board, the student receives a prize. The prize may vary. If the teacher does monthly book orders from the various book clubs, one suggestion is to allow the child to pick a free book from that month's book order. Another suggestion for a prize might be extra time at the library or bookmarks.

> ✓ **Tip:** It is a good idea to keep the READ-O game going for at least two quarters to allow enough time for students to do the reading. If time is limited and conferencing is not an option, simply filling out the book log will be sufficient. Hanging the READ-O boards in the classroom or hallway is an easy way to keep track of students' progress.

Reading Goals

In addition to the reading students will do for the READ-O game, it is helpful for each child to set a reading goal for each school quarter. (See Reading Goal sheet on page 14.) This gives the child something to aim for, as well as some ownership of his or her learning. If time is available, consider setting aside 30 minutes twice a week for uninterrupted free reading time. The purpose for this time is for students to sit anywhere in the room they are comfortable and read a book of their own choice. This is quiet, independent reading time. This time has been labeled as Reading Workshop, DEAR Time (Drop Everything And Read), SIR (Silent Independent Reading), Independent Reading, Silent Reading, and other various titles. This is when students can read READ-O books and work towards their goal. Once a student finishes a book, he or she fills out a book log (pages 12 or 13) and signs up for a conference with you. At the end of the quarter, students who have reached their goal can receive a certificate (page 19).

Establishing some boundaries for goal setting is important. Students in the upper grades cannot, for example, read four picture books in order to make their goal. So consider a limit of one picture book toward a goal. After all, the teacher does not want to discourage reading picture books; they are wonderful! In addition, the number of books for which a student aims needs your approval based on each student's individual reading level. Another important consideration is the number of pages. The teacher may want to consider counting 200-or-more-page books worth two books toward an individual's reading goal.

> ✓ **Tip:** Have one or two large binders with numbered dividers. This is the place students will keep their reading goal sheet and any filled-out reading logs. After the teacher's approval, the student will then file the reading log sheet in the binder behind his or her number. Now the teacher will have all the students' reading organized and in one place.

Game Board

READ-O

My.	NF	SF	Bio.	HF
NF	SF	Bio.	HF	My.
SF	Bio.	HF	My.	NF
Bio.	HF	My.	NF	SF
HF	My.	NF	SF	Bio.

My. = Mystery   NF = Nonfiction   HF = Historical Fiction

SF = Science Fiction   Bio. = Biography

Nonfiction Book Log

Name: _____

Date: _____ Number of Pages: _____

Title: _____

Author: _____

What is the main topic of the book? _____

List facts you learned from the book.

   1. _____

   2. _____

   3. _____

   4. _____

Describe your favorite part of the book.

_____

_____

_____

_____

_____

What other books have you read that are similar to this one?

_____

_____

_____

_____

Fiction Book Log

Name: _____

Date: _____ Number of Pages: _____

Title: _____

Author: _____

List the main characters and their role in the story.

NAME   ROLE IN STORY

_____   _____

_____   _____

_____   _____

_____   _____

Explain the main problem of the story.

_____

_____

_____

How does the story end? How is the problem solved?

_____

_____

_____

Describe your favorite part of the story.

_____

_____

_____

Reading Goal

Student's Name: _____

By _____, my goal is to

(date)

read and understand _____

books. I will use reading time and all

other available times to read my book.

When I finish my book, I must

conference with someone about it and

then record it in my book log.

▪ ▪ ▪ ▪ ▪ ▪ **Rewards** ▪ ▪ ▪ ▪ ▪ ▪

Bonus Box

Compile a list of reward privileges with the help of the class. Some examples include an extra five minutes at the computer, the first to line up, etc. Once a large list is made, put each individual privilege on a fun-shaped card or stationary and laminate it. Place them all in a special box or treasure chest. When students earn a reward, they can draw out three and then choose their favorite from the three. This avoids always giving candy or stickers as a reward.

Personalized Newsletter

Another terrific reward is placing the student's name in the parent newsletter. Make a special section for student news. Using a fun font, type in student names and their special efforts. It is also good to have the students sign their name on the newsletter rather than the teacher typing it.

Student-Selected Rewards

Leave the guesswork out of rewards. Student-selected rewards really motivate kids. After all, they have told the teacher what they want. What better motivation is that? Give the class a few minutes to brainstorm possible, reasonable rewards for themselves. Then have each child tell the teacher two rewards they would like to earn. The teacher will be surprised what really motivates them. Some rewards students tend to choose include the following: 15 minutes at the computer, sit by a friend for the day, wear a baseball cap all day in school, or receive 20 points extra credit in any subject. They are great ideas that do not require any money!

Challenge Plan

Many teachers offer an array of enrichment and/or practice activities for their students in the classroom. However, the problem lies with how to encourage the students to actually do these activities. Using a Challenge Plan is one way to get the students in class organized enough to try them.

A Challenge Plan is a list of all the activities the teacher has set up in the room for the students to do when they finish their work. (See sample on page 17.) Each student receives the list and is in charge of setting up his or her own plan for the quarter. Each student decides which activities he or she wants to do and how many times to do the activity. For example, if a student is interested in Geo-Genius on page 80, he or she will write on the Challenge Plan the number of times he or she plans on doing it.

After everyone has filled in the plan, the teacher needs to collect them, check them over, and sign them. When the teacher checks them over, he or she should ask the following questions for each plan:

- Does this plan fit the ability level of the individual? Are there too many or too few activities?

- Is this plan feasible for the amount of time given to complete it—usually a quarter?

Once the teacher has checked and signed each plan, have each student sign his or her own name. At that point, send the plan home and have each student's parent sign it so the parents are aware of any extra work their child has committed to.

✓ **Tips:** Students should find a special place to keep their plans where they can easily refer to them. Also, keep a copy of each plan for yourself.

Remind students throughout the quarter to complete their plans. Students who complete their plan should be rewarded at the end of the quarter with a certificate or other special reward for all their extra efforts.

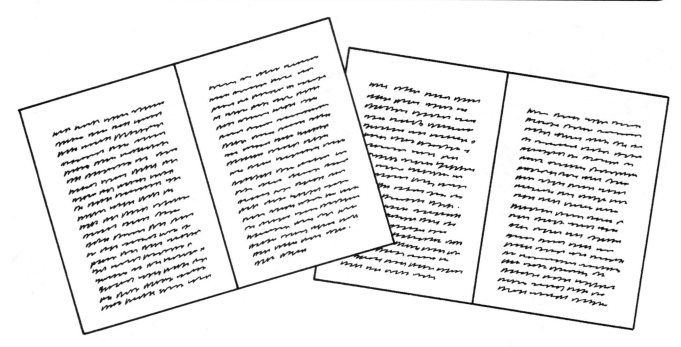

Sample Challenge Plan

Name: _____

Date: _____ Quarter: _____

I agree to complete the following challenge activities before the end of the quarter:

Activity	Number of Times Completed
Whiz Kids	_____
Geo-Genius	_____
Mind Benders	_____
PACK	_____
Calendar Clue	_____
Word of the Week	_____

Teacher Signature: _____

Student Signature: _____

Parent Signature: _____

Certificates

Teachers are often too busy throughout the day to remember to hand out little rewards or certificates to those students who have done something worthy. Usually positive words are the sole way to reinforce positive behavior. However, it is nice for a student to receive something more concrete so they are able to present it to family members with pride. If the teacher cannot hand certificates out regularly, make a point to do so each quarter. On report card day before the teacher hands out the report cards, have a number of certificates to hand out. The teacher can have two or three standard certificates every quarter, but then add new ones and different ones each quarter, as well to keep the surprise. Don't feel every student must get a certificate every quarter. If all students earn certificates, it eliminates the feeling of a reward or "I am special."

Some ideas to use for certificates include the following:
- students who have done the most extra credit
- students who had no late work all quarter
- students who had only one late assignment all quarter
- students who reached their reading goals
- the person who tried the most PACK activities (page 84)
- the person who did the Word of the Week the most often and correctly (page 93)
- students who performed their class job well and regularly
- students with consistently clean desks
- students who are the most improved in a certain area

Every class will most likely be different depending on the activities the teacher has set up in the classroom. Some of the certificates can be followed with an extra reward. For example, the students with no late assignments may get a "no homework" coupon with their certificate. Students with one late assignment will get just the certificate. The teacher can also include a bookmark with the reading goal certificate.

✓ **Tips:** Do not announce to the students what efforts during the quarter will earn certificates. The teacher may want the reward to be given for honest effort and work, not simply to receive a certificate. That's why changing the certificates each quarter, except for a select few, will promote honest efforts.

If the teacher wants to give certificates out more often than once per quarter, a neat trick is to have some generic ones ready. (See page 19 for an award certificate.) Fill in the student's name and your signature ahead of time. Put two in the plan book each week. This will remind the teacher to find something that student did particularly well that week. The certificate is then ready for the teacher anytime. He or she just needs to fill in what the certificate was for.

End-of-the-Year Certificates

In addition to the quarterly certificates, try doing end-of-the-year certificates in which every student receives one. These are fun, personal certificates that reflect something that student may be known for in the classroom. Some of these can be funny as well. Some examples include the following: the most artistic, the trivia guru, or the most improved in a certain area. (*Note:* These categories will change each year depending on the dynamics of the class. This is a fun, positive way to end the school year.)

Fantastic News!

This is to report that

_____ has

_____

_____

Congratulations!

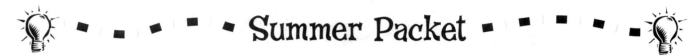

Summer Packet

Many teachers send a letter to their students just before the start of the school year. It's a great way to introduce the teacher and get students excited about the coming year. How about including a small packet of summer activities with that letter? (See sample letter on page 21.)

Pick out your favorite activities from any of the resource books that are fun and cover all subject areas and ability levels. Then students can pick and choose as they see fit. Designate the activities as optional. Those who complete some activities should bring them in the first day of school. They can share special projects if they want, and the teacher can display certain ones. Give every student who participated a certificate as a reward for these extra efforts during the summer.

The teacher can emphasize that the activities can be done with partners or family members. Again, stress that these are optional. They are meant to be fun, yet can be a learning or reviewing experience. Since many children attend camp for the summer, the teacher may want to include one or two activities that tie in—a journal and picture of a favorite camp memory, for example.

✓ **Tips:** It is a good idea to send packets in July, about one month before school, when students may be feeling bored. Make the envelope inviting and exciting. Put stickers on the outside and address it using colorful markers. Include a class list if possible, so students can get together and work on the activities. New friendships may develop before the school year starts.

Sample Summer Letter

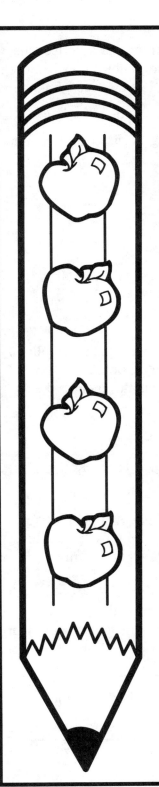

Hello new third grader!

I am so happy you will be part of my class this school year. I certainly hope you had some wonderful experiences this summer and still have a few coming up. No doubt you have thought about school (just a little bit). I remember my summer when I was going into third grade, and at times I felt a little bored and wished school was here. You might even be feeling a little excited and nervous all wrapped up in one.

Well, since we have about four weeks of summer left, I thought I would get you thinking again. I have enclosed some fun activities for you to try over the next few weeks. NO, IT IS NOT HOMEWORK!!! These activities are OPTIONAL, which means you may choose to do as many as you would like. You can do them alone or with some friends. Bring the finished products to school the first few days, and I will display them.

I am looking forward to meeting you and your parents. Enjoy the rest of the summer, and come to Room 27 ready to fill your brain with tons of awesome knowledge.

If you have any questions, email me at ssloan@lom.com.

Sincerely,

Miss Sloan

Goody Bags and Balloons

The beginning of the school year can be frightening for children. A fun way to start off the school year is with a special gift for each student.

On each desk, place a paper lunch sack with a poem or message glued on the front that describes the items in the bag. (See page 23 for a sample poem.) Try to fill the bag with useful items they can use in school. Read the poem together and let the children sift through their bags. It is a nice ice breaker and shows the children your compassion.

The following are examples of some items that may be placed in the goody bags. They can be written with the following clever messages:

- "a pencil to help you create stories"
- "an eraser to help you remember it is all right to make mistakes"
- "a rubber band to help you bounce back from disappointments"
- "a penny for luck"
- "a lollipop to keep you sweet"
- "a bookmark to help you read"

In addition to the bags on the students' desks, have a filled balloon taped to the corner. In the balloon is a message that tells the class one exciting event that will take place that coming school year. The messages are cleverly written so they do not give too many specifics. Some examples include the following:

- "You will eat a spider." (Students will be making spider cookies.)
- "You will rely on your senses." (Students will be blindfolded as part of their Helen Keller unit.)
- "You will create a totem pole." (Students will do a group project for the Native American unit.)

Students will pop their balloons, one at a time, and read the message inside. Know that popping for some may be a bit scary. Suggest to the class ways to pop their balloons. Some options include the following: cutting off the knot with their scissors to allow the balloon to deflate quietly, sitting on it, or poking it with a sharpened pencil (the loudest suggestion).

Now the first day of school becomes a celebration of the year ahead with balloons and goody bags. The teacher can even sprinkle a little confetti on each desk for a festive touch. The students leave that first day excited about the new school year ahead of them!

✓ **Tip:** Roll up the message and stick it in the balloon before you blow it up. Then hang the opened messages in one spot. As the activities unfold, take them down.

Sample Goody Bag Poem

Wow, you've made it
almost to the top.
Kindergarten, 1st grade, 2nd . . .
3rd graders you are not!
Success after success
you've learned but struggled too.
You're a 4th grader now
with new experiences ahead of you!
So here is a pencil,
to help you think and create.
An eraser to remind you
it's ok to make mistakes.
Next, a lollipop to keep you sweet,
for you will be respectful
to other Wilmot kids you meet.
A bookmark,
to mark that special spot.
You'll not only read for fun,
but also to learn a lot.
And last of all,
One coin, shiny and new.
To us you have great value.
There's nothing you can't do!

Homework Buddy

Tired of students consistently forgetting their homework? Try assigning a homework buddy. The teacher does not have to limit it to just those students who always forget. In fact, it is best to give everyone a buddy. The teacher does not want to single anyone out, and hurt feelings will not help students turn in the homework. Partner up the most responsible students with the "not so responsible" students. Give each pair a sticker chart with both names on it. When both students remember their work, the pair gets a sticker. After five stickers (or whatever the teacher decides), the pair is rewarded with a privilege or a "no homework" coupon or whatever reward the teacher chooses.

Have the partners exchange phone numbers so they can call and remind each other. At the end of the day, let the buddies get together to check each other's assignment and/or backpacks to make sure they both have all the books they need for the night. This takes some pressure off the teacher having to constantly remind students.

✓ **Tip:** Emphasize the importance of being respectful if a partner forgets. Tell students that if they cannot work respectfully, they will not participate. When they see the others earning the privileges, they will want to as well. Try switching partners every couple of weeks.

Review Ideas

· Reminder Binder ·

Sometimes we wonder where the school year goes. Time seems to fly. Teachers start to think, "Are the children even aware of all they have learned and experienced by January, or even June for that matter?" To aid their memory, have a reminder binder to browse through throughout the year and especially at the end of the year. It is fun and triggers a lot of memories.

There are several ways of implementing a reminder binder.

1. At the end of each week or day, pick one or two students who will be responsible for choosing one particular event, activity, or lesson. Have them write a brief description and illustrate it (optional) on the pre-made form (page 27) that includes the date, lines for a description, and a box for an illustration. These are then filed in one main binder titled "The Reminder Binder." They should share with the class their choice when they finish.

2. At the end of each month, students brainstorm the month's important events, activities, and lessons. Try to get at least one per student. Write them on the chalkboard. Each student picks one and fills in the pre-made sheet on page 27 and places it in "The Reminder Binder." Students who finish early can do a second one. This repeats monthly.

Both ways get students thinking about what they have learned and experienced, either daily, weekly, or monthly. At the end of the school year, it is exciting to go back and remember all the great learning that took place.

✓ **Tip:** Instead of a binder, students can write their activity on an ice cream scoop shape and build a giant cone that hangs in the room. Any shape will work, such as a train, tree with leaves, or a caterpillar. It is nice to have this visual for quick reference and review.

Reminder Binder Form

_____
Date

[box]

_____

_____

_____

_____

_____

_____

_____
Student Signature

Fortune Teller

A fortune teller game is where the fingers are put in the openings of a folded piece of notebook paper. The paper is then opened and closed the number of times it reads. Underneath each number is a secret message. Now, this game can be turned into a review. The words on the four outside flaps should be content-based words. Instead of numbers on the inside triangular flaps, use "count by's," such as count by 3 up to 21 and count by 5 up to 30, etc. The place for the secret message underneath should now contain a question from the unit being studied with the answer written above it. The kids can partner up and review the unit. They can also hold mini competitions in small groups. Ask one of your students how to make them or see the explanation below and on page 29.

✓ **Tip:** Have the students take out a sheet of paper and you demonstrate how to fold it without telling them why. This really peaks their interest!

Directions

1. Begin with an 8½" x 8½" square piece of paper. 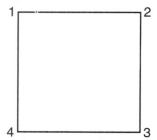	2. Fold corner 3 to corner 1. 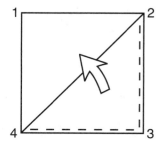	3. Open the folded sheet flat, then fold corner 4 to corner 2. 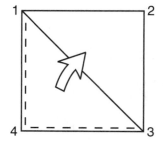
4. Unfold the creased paper. It will look like this. (The dashed lines are the creases.) 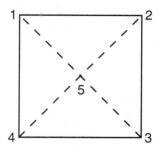	5. Take corner 4 and fold it up to meet number 5. 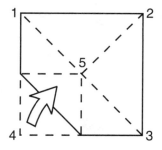	6. Now fold corner 2 to meet number 5. 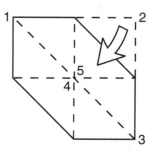

Directions *(cont.)*

7. Follow the same procedure for corners 1 and 3. Your final product will look like this. 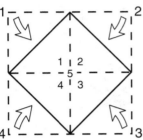	8. Now, with the folds in place, flip over the entire project. 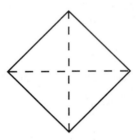
9. Continue folding. Fold corner A to E. Then follow by folding corner B to E, corner C to E, and corner D to E. 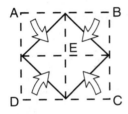	10. After completing the folds, your paper will look like the illustration. (The dashed lines are the folded lines.)
11. Fold in half and then fold in half again. 	12. Unfold the last two folds, so the paper looks like the illustration. 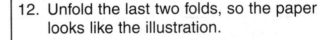
13. Insert one finger under each flap and invert your hand. 	14. Move your fingers apart to open the fortune teller. (You can also use the thumb and forefinger from each hand to open it.) 

Math Review Games

Division Raceway

After learning any multi-step math problem (long division, two-digit numbers times two-digit numbers, etc.), the class will be ready for a high-paced race and challenge. Follow the instructions below.

1. Split your class into teams of about five.

2. The first person on each team writes down the math problem the teacher says.

3. On the teacher's cue, he or she passes the paper to the next teammate who does the first step to the problem.

4. He or she then passes it to the next person who does the second step, and so on until the problem is completed. In most cases, students will receive the math problem more than once depending on the team size and steps to the problem.

5. The team that finishes first and has the correct answer wins the round.

(*Note:* It is very important that each person does only one step. The teacher will need to monitor by walking around and assisting where needed. If a child notices a mistake, he or she can fix it and then do his or her step.)

> ✓ **Tip:** Do two problems on the board together as a whole class, demonstrating what constitutes one step.

No Fear Board Races

The teacher can always do the traditional math races at the board for review and practice. The students still love them, and they work, too. However, some students may be terrified of being in front of the class. A student may know the problem, but may panic because he or she is afraid of making a mistake and possibly being ridiculed. So to ease the student's pain, award two points to the first team that gets it correct and a point to every other team that completes the problem correctly. This way, accuracy is rewarded, not only speed. In addition, give each racer the option to ask his or her next teammate in line to come up and help if he or she is stuck. Eliminating as much fear of embarrassment as possible allows the student at the board to focus on the math and not his or her self-dignity.

Steal the Protractor

Similar to the old time Steal the Bacon game, Steal the Protractor is a fun way for students to practice their mental math.

Directions

1. Split the class into two teams.

2. Stand the two teams in a row facing each other. Leave several feet between teams so the students can run into and out of the center.

3. Place a giant protractor on the ground inbetween the teams. (See game setup below.
   X = Student and P = Protractor) Use any sturdy math tool as a substitute for the protractor.

X		X
X		X
X		X
(Team 1) X	P	X **(Team 2)**
X		X
X		X

4. Secretly give each person a number. The numbers should not be 1–10, but rather numbers that make good answers to various math problems. Some examples of math problems are as follows:

$$9 + 3 = \textbf{12} \qquad 7 \times 2 + 4 = \textbf{18} \qquad 72 \div 9 = \textbf{8} \qquad 4 + 4 \times 3 = \textbf{24}$$

If these were some of the math problems, the student numbers would have to be 12, 18, 8, and 24. Each team has the same set of numbers.

5. Then teacher calls out a math problem, such as 9 + 3. The person on each team whose number matches the math problem's answer, in this case 12, runs into the middle.

   The objective is to steal the protractor and run back to the student's own team without being tagged by the other person on the opposite team. If the student makes it safely back to his or her team with the protractor in hand and without being tagged, the student's team gets a point. If the student is tagged, the tagger's team receives the point. Whoever ends the game with the most points wins.

> ✓ **Tips:** It is best to start off the first set with all the same type of math problems. For example, give all multiplication problems first. Once they understand how to play the game, give more difficult problems.
>
> Have about three math problems with the same answer ready, so each student gets three turns to run into the middle and steal the protractor.
>
> This is also a great game to play outside on the grass. It is a change of pace, and the students get a chance to move around and be active while doing some mental math!

Vital Vocabulary

Vocabulary Bingo

Vocabulary learning can be viewed as boring to some students. A way to spice it up and make it memorable is to play Bingo. Students randomly write down all the vocabulary words for that unit, one word per box. (*Note:* The words can be written on the board so everyone has the same words.)

Read the definition of each word aloud. Students then cover the matching word on the Bingo sheet with a small square of paper, dried bean, or other marker. Once they get a consecutive row, they yell "Bingo" or another word you chose. Pick a word that relates to the unit the class is studying.

Action Vocabulary

Give a set of partners one word from the unit or novel being read. They are to learn the definition and then come up with a simple charade-type action associated with the word. The action should be a clue to the meaning of the word. Once practiced, students share their word, definition, and action with the class. The class then repeats the action. After every two words, go back and review actions and definitions of the previously learned words. The action will help secure the meaning in their minds.

> ✓ **Tip:** Encourage students to keep the actions simple, only one or two movements. Too detailed or lengthy actions will be forgotten. If desired, students can also choose their own words to perform from the unit.

Password

This game is similar to the TV show "Password." It is a terrific way to review vocabulary in the classroom.

Split the class into two teams. The first person from each team comes to the front and sits in the two chairs facing the game show host (the teacher). The game show host begins by giving one-word clues to both players at the same time. The first person to shout out the answer gets two points for the team. For example, the word may be *carnivore*. Possible clues to give are as follows: "animal," "meat," and "teeth." Keep repeating the clues thus far if they are stumped. If still stumped, start giving obvious clues such as "not a herbivore."

As the class sees how this works and gains experience with the clue-giving technique, eventually allow teammates to give clues, one at a time, to their guesser.

Question and Answer

This game is a quick, easy, and fun way to review a short reading in social studies. The game works great for any social studies lesson.

As students read the lesson for that day, they are to write down four questions, the page numbers on which the information is found, and the answers. They should write questions they feel are important facts to remember. Students should not use vocabulary as a question, but should use any information found in the text including graphs, captions, and margin notes as information for their questions. Some practice of this may be necessary. Remember to emphasize finding important information, and not have questions that are trivial.

Reinforce that the goal of the game is to learn the information in a fun, positive way. Having them write questions using the text's margin notes, captions, and graphs teaches the students to look at and read everything on the page, and not just the main text or boldfaced words as they often do.

Split the class in half and give each team an animal name. Pick unique animals to add a fun twist— anteaters and porcupines, for example. The first person on team one asks the first person on team two a question. The answer giver has the following three choices:

1. Answer the question independently (*worth three points*)

2. Answer independently, but using the textbook for help (*worth two points*)

3. Answer using the help of a teammate (*worth one point*)

The answer giver also has a total of 60 seconds to answer the question. He or she can try to answer on his or her own. If the answer is incorrect, he or she can use the remaining time to use the book or team for help.

Next, the second player on team two asks the second player on team one a question from his or her paper. The same procedure as above follows. Do this until each player has had a turn to answer and ask a question. It is fine if the students have similar questions. The repetition only helps ensure learning. Tell the students the word "unfair" will not be spoken (for this one instance anyway). If a team complains of unfairness, penalize that team by subtracting one or more points.

✓ **Tips:** As with all games, the teacher should be the official judge and timekeeper. The teacher can also collect all the questions and ask the questions to make the game run a bit smoother.

Smart Sack

Usually, some parents mention the need for more homework or more practice in certain subjects, such as math or reading. The Smart Sack will help avoid some of these requests. Fill a cheap shoulder strap bag or backpack with fun, challenging, and review activities for kids to do alone and/or with family members.

Let the child take the bag home for three or more days. When time is up, they bring it back with the journal page filled in. (See page 35.) It then is sent home with the next student for three days. There is also the option to send one sack for boys and one for girls for ease in recordkeeping. Other ideas include odd numbers and even numbers, a simple random drawing with a check-off sheet, or splitting the class into two parts. Use as many sacks as you like. Remember, the more Smart Sacks, the more materials the teacher will need. Three Smart Sacks is a good amount.

A sample sack can include the following:

- one or two math games to be played with family members

- flash cards—math, states, sight word vocabulary, time, capitals, etc.

- fun work sheets that cover any subject

- trivia questions

- two books—one nonfiction, one fiction or poetry

- logic puzzles or 3-D puzzles

- a list of materials with a parent signature sheet to show they have seen it and checked that all materials are present

- a brief questionnaire or journal so each student can report back about what activities he or she used

---

✓ **Tips:** The contents can change as needed. For example, always keep two books so the materials list does not need to be changed, but change the books to fit topics being taught. The same goes with flash cards. If the class is studying capitals, make sure the capital flash cards are in the sack.

Within the sack, have a wide range of ability levels. Some students may need the addition flash cards, while others may use the multiplication. Some students may need sight word vocabulary, while others may not.

Smart Sack Letter

Smart Sack

My child used the Smart Sack and all the materials are present that are listed on the attached paper.

_____

Parent Signature

- -

I used the Smart Sack. Two activities I did include the following:

1. _____

2. _____

My favorite part of the Smart Sack was _____

_____

_____

My least favorite part of the Smart Sack was _____

_____

_____

Something I would like to see added to the Smart Sack is _____

_____

_____

I checked the Smart Sack and all the materials are present that are listed on the attached paper.

_____

Student Signature

Roulette Review

When it comes time to review for main tests in subjects, such as science or social studies, it is refreshing to review the material the day before the test in a game format. Roulette Review is a game that uses cooperative teamwork with the chance for winning based mainly on luck.

Directions

1. To begin the game, divide the class into four teams with approximately five people per team.

2. Each team must decide on who will be the official speaker. The speaker is the only person to whom the teacher will listen. The speaker repeats the team's answers (not his or her own).

3. Team One is asked a question.

4. If Team One answers correctly, they pick a chip out of a bag. The bag should contain 24 roulette chips (more or less depending on the amount of questions the teacher may have). The chip picked will have the amount of points earned for that question. The points can vary in amounts ranging from 50 to 5,000. However, in the bag there are five "Bonk" roulette chips. If the team picks a chip that says "Bonk" in red letters, the team loses ALL its total points earned thus far. If the team picks a black "Bonk" chip, it loses only half of its total points. If the team does not have any points and picks a "Bonk" chip (red or black), it is now at negative 200 points.

    If Team One is asked a question and answers it incorrectly, the same question goes to Team Two. If they cannot answer it, the question moves onto Team Three and then Four, etc.

    If no team can answer the question, review the answer briefly with the class and then throw out the question. It is now Team Two's turn to be asked a question, even if they answered Team One's question correctly.

    (*Note:* Once a team has answered correctly, they must decide before they pick a chip if they are going to accept the chip or give the chip to another team. If they decide to give the chip away, they must state aloud which team will be given the chip.)

    The teacher is the official judge. If a team argues with the judge's decision or displays poor sportsmanship, the team will automatically lose 200 points. This is why the speaker's role is very important. Once the team has decided the answer, the speaker must relay the answer to the teacher. The speaker is also the person who tells the teacher whether the team will accept the chip to be picked or give it away.

✓ **Tip:** Have more red-colored "Bonk" chips than black. If the class plays enough or with older students, it is smart to vary the amount of "Bonk" chips (red or black) used in each game. This will avoid teams knowing the amount of "Bonk" chips left.

Parent Involvement Ideas

"The Bonus Brief" Newsletter

Most teachers agree that newsletters are vital to home/school communication. However, most teachers can also agree that they can be very time consuming and, in some cases, stressful to write. An easy way to complete a newsletter without taking a lot of time is to do a weekly briefing. This is a simple recap of the key learning events.

Under each day write one or two sentences that explain one or two important learning activities that took place that day. Fill out the sheet daily and send it home on Friday. (See page 39 for newsletter.) It is then the parent's job to ask their child about those events.

This "brief" newsletter serves several purposes. First, it communicates to the parents what learning is taking place each week. Second, it serves as a review for the student. Third, it promotes parent/child communication. No longer does the parent ask, "What did you do in school this week?" and the child responds, "Nothing."

There is also a special place to add in any important dates and upcoming events, as well as who celebrated a birthday that week. Parents and children love to see their names in print. Also, add a place to write names of students who have had special successes that week. For example, "Congratulations to Betty B. and Jay C.—our class spelling bee winners!"

If the teacher does The Word of the Week activity on page 93, there is a spot to write it.

> ✓ **Tip:** It is helpful to always copy the newsletter on the same colored paper. This will make it easier for parents to locate the letter in the child's home folder or backpack.

The Bonus Brief

Week of _____

Ask your child about the following days:

Monday

Tuesday

Wednesday

Thursday

Friday

Special Dates/Notes: _____

_____

_____

Word of the Week	Birthdays

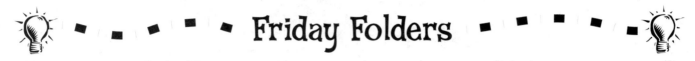

Friday Folders

An easy way to keep parents involved in their child's progress and students aware of their own progress is to have a weekly form filled out by the teacher and the student. This form can be placed in a special folder to be carried back and forth from school to home. (See sample on page 41.)

At the end of each week, students write down their progress and other school-related events. Ideas to include are late assignments, reminders, special events, etc. It is placed in the folder, sent home for parents to read, sign, and write comments or questions if they want.

The teacher's role is to glance at each student's thoughts and make suggestions for additions. The teacher also writes comments about the student. However, since time is limited, it is suggested that the teacher comment only on a small group of students each week. So every student will end up with one comment from the teacher each month. For example, if you have 24 students, each Friday you will write in six students' folders. Number one through six will get comments the first week, seven through twelve the next week, and so on. Meanwhile, each student fills out the form every Friday and returns the signed form and folder to the teacher on Monday.

✓ **Tip:** Have all students use the same color folder labeled with their name and teacher's name. This will make it easier in collecting and locating the folders.

Weekly Comment & Reflection Form

Parents, please read and sign below your child's comments. Your own comments are optional. I will fill out a comment box monthly.

Name: _____ Date: _____

Student Comments: _____

_____

_____

_____

Special Events: _____

_____

Achievements: _____

_____

Behavior: _____

_____

Student Signature: _____

Parent Signature: _____

Parent Comments *(optional)*: _____

_____

_____

Teacher Signature: _____

Teacher Comments *(optional)*: _____

_____

_____

Gathering the Pieces

The parents of students are great resources of information. It is a good idea to find out as much information from them as possible before the school year has started or before any problems occur. Send a letter expressing your interest in getting to know each child's strengths and weaknesses in the areas of physical, academic, social, and emotional growth. (See sample letter on page 43.) Also, inquire if the child has received any type of special service in the past (gifted programs, learning disability programs, etc.). Parents generally will welcome the opportunity to speak about their child. It also helps them feel secure that the teacher knows the needs of their child right away.

It is important, too, that the teacher state in the letter that the information they are providing will be absolutely confidential and will not be placed in their child's permanent file. Parents will feel more comfortable telling confidential information if they do not need to worry where the information will be placed.

Parents can mail the response back to the teacher or put it in the school mailbox at the start of the year. Generally, it is not wise to have the child bring it in. But if the teacher asks them to put it in a sealed envelope, it is usually not a problem. Students are turning in so many forms the first day that they are not likely to be curious about its contents.

✓ **Tips:** Keep a binder and put all the responses inside alphabetically for easy reference. Highlight any bit of information that needs to stand out and be remembered.

Keep the note general, allowing parents to write as much as they feel comfortable. Ask them to speak about the four main areas mentioned above and anything else they feel is pertinent to the education of their child.

Sample Parent Letter

Dear Parents,

Welcome to fourth grade! Some of you have had other children go through fourth grade before at Wilmot Elementary and others are first-timers. We are excited to meet all of you and use you as a helpful resource in the classroom.

In order for us to better understand your child's physical, social, emotional, and academic characteristics and needs, it would be very helpful if you would keep us informed about any particular situation or condition that could affect school behavior. Thoughts you have about your child's school experience would also be appreciated.

If you would, please take a moment now and write down any information you feel is necessary for us to better understand and educate your child. You are a valuable resource for us. Without your input, we only have some of the pieces of the puzzle. Working with your child will give us a great deal of information about him or her. However, we feel it is very beneficial to be informed at the start of the school year.

As you write this information, keep in mind the characteristics listed above (physical, social, emotional, and academic), and please make mention of any extra school services your child has received in the past.

Please note that any information that is received by you will be absolutely confidential. It will not be placed in you child's permanent file.

Sincerely,

Mrs. Zurim

Mrs. Zurim

You can mail this form to me at Wilmot Elementary School (795 Wilmot Road), deliver it to school in a sealed envelope via your child, or place it in Mrs. Zurim's school mailbox. Use the back of this sheet for your response or attach a separate paper. Please return by August 31.

Parent's Name: _____

Child's Name: _____

Book-'N-Bag-It Lunch

A great way to keep close touch with classroom parents is to invite them in for a Book-'N-Bag-It Lunch. This is an informal, casual way to say "hello" and remind the teacher once again which student belongs to whom.

Invite the parents of students into the classroom at lunchtime. (See sample letter on page 45.) During this time, parents and students sit together and eat a sack lunch brought from home and read together. Place tablecloths or giant fabric pieces on the floor and desks. Small groups can have an indoor picnic while enjoying a book the child or parent picked. It is cozy and fun. The teacher can also provide dessert if he or she so desires. Having one Book-'N-Bag-It Lunch per quarter seems to work well.

Sometimes instead of reading together, students can share their portfolio with their parents or stories they have written that quarter. If the students have recently created mini skits for a novel unit, this is a wonderful opportunity to share those with the parents as well.

For those students whose parent(s) cannot attend, have them invite another relative. Otherwise, they can eat with the teacher or join up with classroom friends.

✓ **Tips:** Send home a notice two weeks prior to the lunch so parents can arrange work schedules. In addition, have them RSVP, so the teacher will know which students will be eating without parents and can make accommodations.

Book-'N-Bag-It Letter

Dear Parents,

It is time for a Book-'N-Bag-It Lunch! On _____, you are invited to our classroom, Room _____, to read and eat lunch with your child.

Please be at the classroom at _____ till _____.

Bring a simple sack lunch and drink from home along with your favorite book. You will sit with your child, eat lunch, and read a favorite book. Your child can pick a book from school, too. Your child may also be sharing his or her creative stories or portfolio. Dessert will be provided.

If you are unable to attend, any other adult family member may attend in your place. Otherwise, your child will be welcomed to eat with friends and their parents or myself. Please know that there will be other Book-'N-Bag-It Lunches throughout the year for you to attend.

Please fill out the bottom portion and return it to school by _____.

Sincerely,

_____

- -

Please check your response below.

_____ Yes, I will be attending.

_____ No, I cannot attend.

Child's Name _____

Parent Signature _____

Open House Activities

Inviting parents into the classroom is something every teacher faces. It is fun to have activities set up in the room for two reasons. One reason is to keep parents occupied and having a fun time. The second reason is to show the parents that the teacher can be creative, fun, and willing to do some unique activities with the children.

Silhouettes

A few days before parents are expected to come to the classroom, draw a silhouette of each student. Have an independent activity planned to keep students busy while the teacher or parent helper takes one child at a time to trace his or her silhouette. Sit the student on a tall chair, preferably with a back on it, for students to lean against. The back prevents movement. Hang black construction paper on the chalkboard and shine a light onto the student's profile. Using a pencil, chalk, or marker, trace the shadow of the student's profile. Be sure to write the student's name on the back of the black paper.

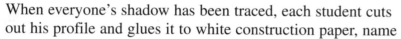

When everyone's shadow has been traced, each student cuts out his profile and glues it to white construction paper, name side down. Again, his or her name goes on the back, but this time on the white paper. When finished, he or she writes a brief description of himself or herself to be stapled onto the bottom of the picture. Descriptions can include the child's likes or dislikes, special talents, facts about his family, and/or special features. Hang each silhouette up so parents can go around the room and find their child.

Estimation Jars

An estimation jar is a sealed, clear container filled to the rim with any item (cotton balls, jelly beans, etc.). People then estimate the number in the container and write their guess on a piece of paper. The closest estimate without going over wins the container's contents. It is the winner's turn to fill it up for the next round.

Have some student-created estimation jars for the parents to estimate. The next day, the students will have fun seeing what their parents' guesses were and who won. Use this activity only if the class has studied estimation.

Word Search

Make a word search using all of the students' first names. If possible, enlarge the word search with a poster machine. Hang it up in the room and ask the parents to try and find their child's name. Keep a few highlighters handy for parents to use.

Self-Esteem Ideas

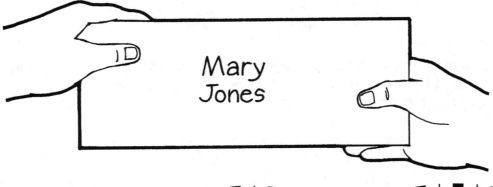

Thankful Thoughts

Get students' parents involved in boosting their child's self-esteem. Send a secret note home to each child's parents with three cute cutout figures inside. (See sample letter on page 49.) In the note, ask parents to jot down three things for which they are thankful about their child.

Have them focus on the character of the student, such as "I am thankful for the way you offer to read aloud to your baby brother each night" or "I am thankful for the hard work you put forth in your daily chores at home. You really help me out a lot." Make sure the parent writes his or her child's name before each compliment and signs it—one compliment per cutout.

Ask the parents to send the compliments back in a sealed envelope by a given date. When every child has three compliments from his or her parents, then pass them out.

The following idea is a fun way to distribute them:

1. Just before school, give each child two of their three cutouts.

2. Give the third cutout to another student.

3. When the children come in, they will have three complimentary cutouts on their desks.

4. Explain that each of them has one cutout that is not theirs and to leave it on his or her desk. The idea is to have each student go to the front of the room and read aloud the other classmate's compliment from their family and then give it to him or her. This way the whole class gets to hear one compliment for every child. It is fun and the students are very surprised.

> ✓ **Tip:** Read the compliments before passing them out. Choose wisely the compliments to be read aloud. You do not want to embarrass anyone.

Thankful Thoughts Letter

Dear Parents,

Shhhhhh! It is a secret!

You are going to have a terrific opportunity to build up your child's self-esteem. Please write three things about your child for which you are thankful on the enclosed cutouts. Write one thankful thought on each cutout. Other family members may participate, too.

Please return the cutouts to me in a sealed envelope with your child by _____. My goal is to display them in the classroom as a surprise to the children when they return.

Recognizing the goodness in your child's character rather than his or her performance is very rewarding to him or her. It is important to put your child's name on each "thankful thought" pattern. Here are some examples of thoughts you might write:

- _____ *(student's name)* _____, I am thankful for your helpfulness. There are many times when I am very busy, and you have helped me without complaining.

- _____ *(student's name)* _____, I am thankful for your creativity. I would miss out on a lot of enjoyment if I didn't hear your thoughtful ideas or share in one of your projects.

- _____ *(student's name)* _____, I am thankful for your kindness. I appreciate you helping your younger brother with his math.

Your compliments to your child will be displayed. Consequently, it is very important that every child have three "thankful thoughts." I thank you in advance for the time and thoughtfulness this activity requires. I believe your child will feel extra special after reading your words.

Sincerely,

_____

Name Pass

Give your students compliments they will always remember and can keep close at hand. Follow the directions below.

1. Put each student's name on separate letter-size envelope.

2. Hand each student his or her envelope, as well as the blank compliment slips. (See page 51.) The teacher chooses the amount that he or she deems suitable.

3. Each child then passes only his or her envelope to the person seated on his or her left.

4. This is where the compliments begin. Each student writes one positive statement about the person whose name appears on the envelope and slips the written compliment into the envelope.

5. On the teacher's cue, students pass again to the left and write a compliment to the person on this next envelope, and so on, until each student receives his or her envelope back.

6. Now, instead of the envelope being empty, it is filled with kindness.

7. The last person to receive the envelope should seal it before handing it to the owner.

8. At this point, emphasize these are their personal compliments and should not be opened in school. Suggest they take them home and enjoy reading them in a quiet spot.

✓ **Tips:** Envelopes work best, because it keeps students from reading others' comments and copying what has been said. Instead, students are apt to comment on something he or she truly feels about that person.

The teacher can add a compliment to each envelope as well. Make sure everyone signs his name for accountability, and make sure the compliments focus on the person's character, not physical appearance.

Another tip is to put desks in a large circle or U-shape to ease the confusion of passing the envelopes.

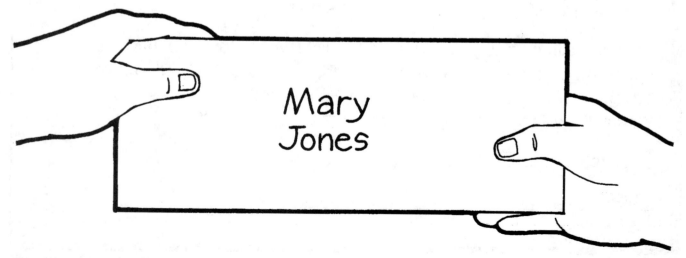

Name Passes

Dear _____,

You are _____

_____

Signed: _____

Dear _____,

You are _____

_____

Signed: _____

Dear _____,

You are _____

_____

Signed: _____

Dear _____,

You are _____

_____

Signed: _____

Valentines to Your Partner

Another great way to get students to think about the individuality of their classmates is to write a complimentary valentine to a given partner. One partner might be their editing partner. This is the person with whom they have been working side by side editing, reading, and sharing stories. It helps having the students write to a person with whom they have worked often, because, if they are struggling for compliments, they can always mention what a great writer, editor, or idea maker the person is. By February, it is late enough in the year so that students know each other well and have had many experiences working with one another.

The idea is to have them create a valentine with decorations and, most importantly, a short poem, paragraph, jingle, etc., about their partner. When everyone is finished, they will be read in front of the class. Either the person who made the valentine can read it aloud, or he can pick a friend to read it for him. Some students may need encouragement from the teacher to read aloud. However, most of the time they will choose to read their own work themselves. Once a few students set the example, everyone else usually follows.

✓ **Tip:** It is important to read the valentines aloud to further instill the wonderful compliments being read. It also gives credibility when they are shared aloud. Keep the mood of this activity light and fun.

 # Lines and Celebrations

Line Up

Teachers are always looking for a unique way to get students to line up. For example, the teacher may ask, "Anyone with three vowels in your name line up."

How about having the students compliment each other before they step into line? One at a time, a child turns to his or her left and says one compliment about the child seated there. Then the student lines up. The child who received the compliment turns to the left and says something nice about that person and so on until everyone is in line.

The teacher should start modeling for students how to make a good compliment. For the first time, accept all compliments as they are. After that, tell them that the compliments cannot be about physical features, but instead about the person's character. Younger students may need examples. Older students catch on quickly.

✓ **Tip:** After receiving the compliment, all students in line must be quiet and listen to the other compliments being said. If it is a problem, have talking students sit back down and wait until all compliments are given.

Let's Celebrate

Is it time the teacher gave students some individual acknowledgement—telling them how wonderful they are? Choose a student for the day and celebrate that child. Follow the instructions below.

1. Pick about four weeks during the year, maybe a time when the teacher is feeling the class is lacking in self-esteem.

2. Each day randomly pick a child, and put a balloon on his or her desk. As students enter, they will quickly identify the student of the day by the balloon.

3. Fill out a Student-of-the-Day certificate and add some special comments from you about his or her unique qualities.

4. Place a sticky note on everyone's desk.

5. Have each student write a compliment on the sticky note and put it on the Student of the Day's desk.

✓ **Tips:** Hang the Student-of-the-Day certificate on the board, so the other children can read the nice comments the teacher had to say about that child. In addition, write his or her name on the board in colorful letters above the certificate. The teacher can also give the student special privileges throughout the day, such as lining up first, calling others to line up, or doing a special job that students enjoy.

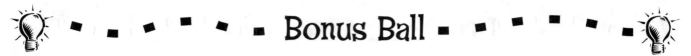

Bonus Ball

The first week of school, teachers spend time with activities that help the students get acquainted. This activity will help the teacher achieve that goal. Follow the directions below.

1. Write several questions concerning things about which you are curious. Write the questions on a ball. Some sample questions include the following:

   • Tell one thing you are worried about this school year.

   • Tell about a time you forgot your homework. What happened?

   • Name someone in the room you would like to get to know better.

   • Who was your teacher last year?

   • What is one unique quality you have?

2. The students sit in a circle and toss the ball around the circle. To get the students learning names, require them to say the name of the person to whom they are tossing the Bonus Ball. This also alleviates any confusion about who was supposed to get the ball if it is accidentally thrown astray.

3. The question the child's left thumb lands on is the one he or she reads aloud and answers. The teacher can also split the class into two groups so more students can participate.

4. After students have received the ball and shared, they should sit on their hands. The ball can only be thrown then to those with hands in the air, alleviating any one person getting the ball over and over.

✓ **Tip:** An extension to this activity may be to cover the ball with math equations or story problems. The ball is tossed in the same manner, but instead the student is answering a math problem.

Behavior Management Ideas

If the Teacher wins:
_____
_____
_____

If the Students win:
_____
_____
_____

After-Work Reflection

When students spend time doing a project either alone or with a group, often one important element of their learning is left out. That element is reflection. Reflecting on what has been done is a major part of learning. The reflection sheet on page 57 is designed to not only help the student remember what he or she did, but also to help the student understand how the current experience will help him or her. These questions are designed in a way that there is not a correct answer. They are open-ended to fit each individual's own experiences.

If the reflection is done in the same manner and for every project, it may become monotonous to the students. Remember to have students reflect on only those activities the teacher feels need reflection. In addition, have students reflect in a variety of ways. Using the same questions, students can write their answers, whisper their thoughts to a partner, or share their thoughts with the class by going around in a circle.

✓ **Tip:** Hang up a poster with the questions for easy referral. Students can then use the questions to foster a quick class discussion.

After-Work Reflection Form

Name: _____ Date: _____

1. What was I asked to do?

_____

_____

2. What did I do well?

_____

_____

_____

3. What did I find more difficult or challenging?

_____

_____

_____

4. Next time I do a similar project, what will I do differently?

_____

_____

_____

5. I liked or disliked this project because _____

_____

_____

_____

_____

_____

_____

_____

 # Behavior Reflection

If a student forgets his or her homework, a teacher may have the student stay in at recess or during study hall, do the missing work, and fill out a behavior reflection form. (See page 59.) This form is designed to have students think about what they did, why it was inappropriate, and how to avoid this behavior next time. They need to answer in complete sentences and thoughtfully. This form is then taken home that evening, signed by the student's parents, and brought back to school the next day. It is a great way to keep parents informed of late work and a great way to keep the student on track of his or her responsibilities.

This form is only effective for those students who forget occasionally. For the repeat offender, other measures will have to be taken to better help him or her remember. Also, the reflection form is general enough that it can also be used for other situations, such as a social problem that occurred that day in school. Filling out a sample reflection form together, as a whole class, would be a good way to model what is expected of the students.

If the teacher does not have a study hall, consider getting some teachers in the same grade level to give up one lunch period to sit for study hall. Study hall duty would be on a rotating basis. The more teachers involved, the fewer lunches missed per teacher. If this is not possible, the student should stay in from recess to fill out the reflection form and do the missing work.

✓ **Tip:** The teacher may want to have a spot on the chalkboard or a small dry erase board for those students who are to go to study hall that day. This will also serve as a reminder to the teacher and the students that they have a reflection form needing to be signed. It is suggested to use their student numbers rather than names on this board to avoid embarrassment.

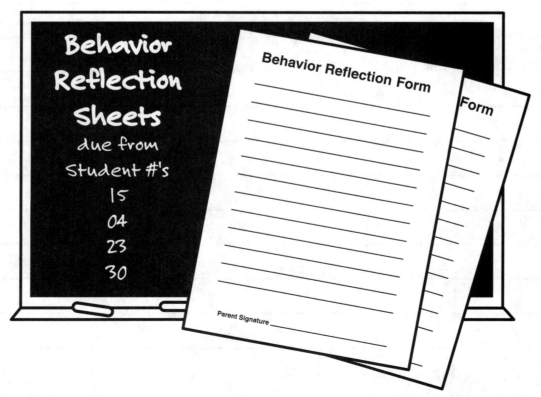

Behavior Reflection Form

Name: _____ Date: _____

Please answer in complete sentences using your best writing.

1. What did I do?

   _____

   _____

   _____

2. How often does this happen? Circle one.

          very often   sometimes   rarely

3. Why was this inappropriate? What problems did it cause?

   _____

   _____

   _____

4. Two things I will do differently next time to help me are the following:

   _____

   _____

Teacher Signature: _____

Teacher Comments (optional): _____

_____

_____

_____

Parent Signature: _____

Parent Comments (optional): _____

_____

_____

_____

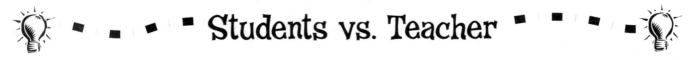

Students vs. Teacher

Decide one skill with which the class, as a whole, needs practice. The skill—listening to directions—is a favorite among many teachers for this game.

Find some game pieces and make a game board of some kind with the skill written at the top. (See the sample on page 61.) Hang it in the room. With the teacher's approval, the class decides on a reward if they win. Then the teacher picks the reward if he or she wins. These are clearly decided, written down, and posted on the end of the game board. The teacher can decide how long to run the game. The longer the teacher wants to play, the longer the game board will have to be. A week is usually an ample amount of time.

State the following rules: In order for the class to move their game piece, they must successfully and accurately retell the directions that were previously given. If the three people called on cannot repeat the directions accurately, the teacher gets to move his or her piece.

The following is an example: Give specific directions on an activity the students are about to start. Say, "Write three math problems using the factors 3, 7, and 21. Put your name on your paper, the date, and put it into your portfolio." After the directions have been given and the class understands them to the best of their ability, call on three people to repeat the directions. If any one of the three makes a mistake, the teacher gets to move his or her game piece. Otherwise, the class moves their game piece ahead toward their reward.

✓ **Tip:** Keep it light and fun, not to embarrass anyone. Wait until all three students have repeated the directions before stating whether it is right or wrong. Chances are the class will know right away if a mistake has been made.

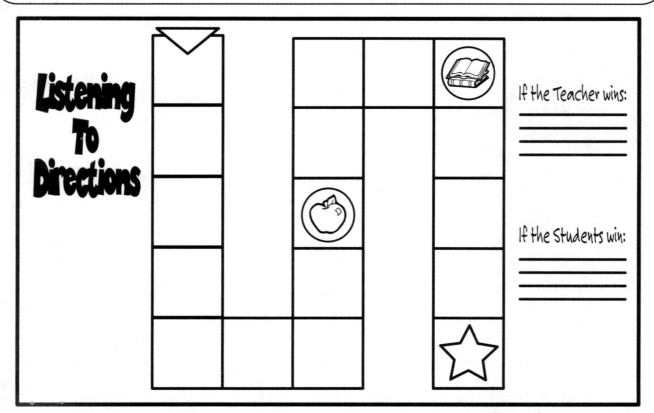

Game Board and Pawns

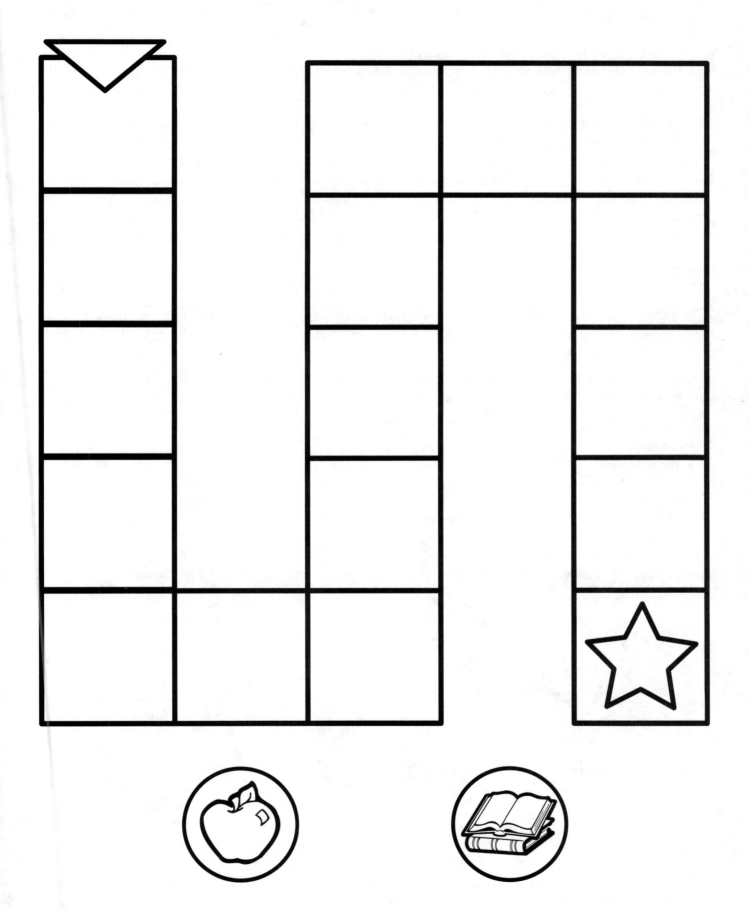

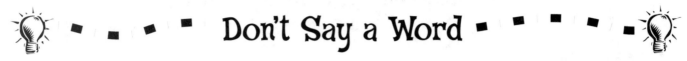

Don't Say a Word

Tired of telling the class to be quiet in the halls? Use this activity to keep noise to a minimum without having to speak.

Simply hand the talking child a "Shh Ticket." Use any fun shapes or the ones provided on page 63. Write "Shh" on them, and laminate them. Keep them by the door in an envelope marked "Shh Tickets." Take the envelope every time the teacher and the class leave, to remind students to be quiet in the hall. To implement the "Shh Tickets," hand out a ticket to whoever is talking in the hall. The teacher should not even need to say a word to the child. This way the teacher is not speaking in the hall either. Students put the tickets back when they return to the classroom. The consequence can vary. For example, the teacher may elect to have any student who gets a ticket lose five minutes of recess.

✓ **Tips:** Keep a sticky note pad and pencil in the envelope to write down the child's name so the teacher will not forget who received a ticket in case they lose it. (They usually remind the teacher anyway.)

Pull out one ticket just before the teacher leaves the room to make it visible for the students. It is a nice reminder and lets the children know the teacher is prepared to give a ticket.

Shh Tickets

 # Secret Workers

Need a new strategy to get your students to stay quiet and focus on their work? Have Secret Workers. Secretly pick two people and write their names down. Announce to the class that the teacher has picked two Secret Workers. If the two Secret Workers are quiet, follow the directions, and stay on task, they will earn a reward for the entire class. If the two do not behave properly, the class will not receive the reward. Since no one knows who the Secret Workers are, everyone is forced to behave as the teacher has asked. This behavior system works well for shorter lengths of time—about half-hour to 40-minute time frames.

Rewards can be anything the teacher chooses, such as five extra minutes of recess, free time, stickers, etc. Extra recess is a logical reward. The teacher can always say, "Since you used the class time so well and stayed on task, we will have extra time to get in more recess." Or the teacher might say, "Since you have worked so hard, you have earned an extra five minutes of break time."

There can be variations to the Secret Workers. One variation is to tell the class that the teacher will be picking one boy and one girl. Another variation is to divide the class in half, and tell the class that one person will be picked from the left side of the room and one from the right side. After using this technique several times, the teacher can then have a competition between the two groups.

✓ **Tips:** If the Secret Workers are successful, be sure to announce their names and have the class thank them. If the Secret Workers are unsuccessful, talk to them personally and do not reveal the names to the class.

It is a good idea to announce aloud how the Secret Workers are doing. For example, a teacher might say, "Wow, the Secret Workers are doing really well" or "Uh-oh, our Secret Workers need to be careful."

Classroom Management Ideas

Idea Box

For creative writing sessions, consider having an idea box handy. This is a tool for any student struggling for a topic to write about. The box can be any box that is available—a shoebox decorated with the words "Idea Box" stuck on in large colorful letters is one possibility. Inside this box are story starters written on rectangle-shaped pieces of colorful paper. Have them laminated to keep them durable over the years.

Some of the ideas include the following:

- Oh my, I just woke up with an extra eyeball!
- I just won the lottery!
- What would it be like to be a gum ball?
- Help, I'm only two inches tall!

- My neighbor is a genie.
- I have three wishes.
- The day I broke my arm . . .

These ideas should be a mix—from wild and weird to serious and real—to tap into all types of children's thinking styles. Also, include pictures found from magazines that would spark the imagination. One example of a picture is an advertisement for crayons. The sentence starter might say, "It has millions of crayons on a path that goes on forever" or "It is colorful and mysterious."

> ✓ **Tip:** The teacher can make a rule that the student must pick three without looking and choose one from those three. This is helpful when a student who is trying to avoid writing and decides to thumb through the entire box "looking" for that exact one. Or, the teacher can give a time limit for choosing an idea using a timer.

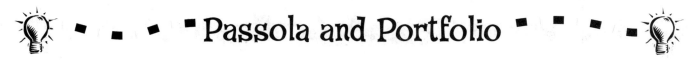

Passola and Portfolio

Passola

Need a fun way to spice up the old boring routine of passing out books at the start of the school year? Try Passola! Students will beg to do it throughout the year.

If books are labeled with student names or student numbers, pile them up on the first student's desk. That student starts to pass the books down the row one at a time. Students continue passing books down the rows, continuously one after the other, without throwing, dropping, or piling. When they see their own book, they take it and pass on the others. At one point, it should flow with all the books in motion, with the end result of everyone having his or her own book.

> ✓ **Tip:** Before starting, quickly review the path the books should be passed to avoid confusion during the activity. Start passing in different spots in the room. It does not have to be at the end of a row or group. This way the person who sits at the end is not always left out of the passing.

The Easy Portfolio

This activity works for both the avid classroom portfolio keeper and for those trying to start a portfolio collection in their classroom. Follow the directions below.

1. Start a basic portfolio with a typical pocket folder. Students can decorate them and then place them in hanging files in a large crate under their student names.

2. At the beginning of the year, ask each student to sign their name in their neatest handwriting on a piece of paper. If the student has learned cursive, then the name must be in cursive.

3. Next, have them create and accurately solve the most difficult math problem they can think of on another paper.

4. Last, students should write three or four school-related goals.

5. Date all the papers and put them in the portfolio.

6. Take a photograph of each student and add the picture to the portfolio. These items will stay in the portfolio all year.

7. At the end of the year, repeat all three writing activities, as well as take another photograph.

8. Set aside time for the students to now compare them. The teacher and the students will be amazed at the growth shown from these three simple activities. In addition, have students take a look at the two photographs. They will be surprised to see their own physical changes. This is a fun, concrete way to demonstrate that they have in fact grown in one school year.

Parent/Teacher Conferences

Pre-Conference Questionnaire

Parent conferences can be a stressful time, especially if the teacher is unsure what to expect from an individual conference. One way to keep the parent focused, help the teacher prepare, and ward off unexpected questions is to have a pre-conference questionnaire. (See page 69 for a sample.) The questionnaire should be sent home about two weeks prior to the conference date and sent back to the teacher a week before the conference date. This will give the teacher enough time to prepare and gather information needed to answer questions thoroughly.

> ✓ **Tip:** Have the sheet at the conference to refer back to. It will help refresh the parents' memory of issues they mentioned.

Student Questionnaire

Parents are usually very interested in their child's social life at school. They may wonder, "Does my child fit in? Does my child have a friend to play with or be a partner with? What does my child do at recess?" In order to accurately answer these questions and other social questions, it is helpful to go directly to the child for the answer.

A week before conferences, ask the students to fill out the questionnaire as truthfully and accurately as they can. (See page 70 for a sample.) Tell them this is confidential and should not be discussed with anyone. This will help avoid hurt feelings and will promote honest answers.

Student Self-Evaluation

One additional form to have filled out for conferences is a student self-evaluation sheet. (See page 71.) This will give the teacher and the parents insight on how the student views himself or herself. This will also promote discussion between the teacher and the student about specific areas. For example, if a student scores himself inappropriately high or particularly low on a certain question, that is the time to discuss it.

Bring this sheet to the conference and review it together. Since the teacher has already clarified with the child any extreme scoring, the teacher will be able to now explain it to the parents. By using these sheets, the teacher will not only be very prepared, but will appear competent. Having insight to a child will promote trust between the teacher and the parents.

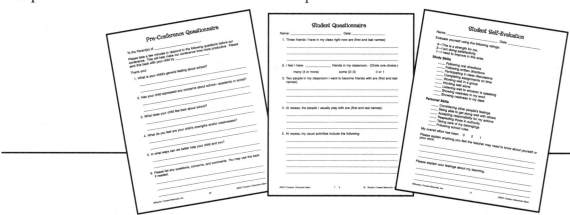

Pre-Conference Questionnaire

To the Parent(s) of _____,

Please take a few minutes to respond to the following questions before our conference. This will help make our conference time more productive. Please send this back with your child by _____.

Thank you!

1. What is your child's general feeling about school?

    _____

    _____

2. Has your child expressed any concerns about school—academic or social?

    _____

    _____

3. What does your child like best about school?

    _____

    _____

4. What do you feel are your child's strengths and/or weaknesses?

    _____

    _____

5. In what ways can we better help your child and you?

    _____

    _____

6. Please list any questions, concerns, and comments. You may use the back if needed.

    _____

    _____

    _____

Student Questionnaire

Name: _____ Date: _____

1. Three friends I have in my class right now are (first and last names):

   _____

   _____

   _____

2. I feel I have _____ friends in my classroom. (Circle one choice.)

   many (4 or more)   some (2–3)   0 or 1

3. Two people in my classroom I want to become friends with are (first and last names):

   _____

   _____

   _____

4. At recess, the people I usually play with are (first and last names):

   _____

   _____

   _____

5. At recess, my usual activities include the following:

   _____

   _____

   _____

   _____

   _____

Student Self-Evaluation

Name: _____ Date: _____

Evaluate yourself using the following ratings:

3—This is a strength for me.
2—I am doing satisfactorily.
1—I need to improve in this area.

Study Skills

_____ Following oral directions
_____ Following written directions
_____ Participating in class discussions
_____ Completing assignments on time
_____ Working well in a group
_____ Working well alone
_____ Listening well to whoever is speaking
_____ Showing neatness in my work
_____ Showing neatness in my desk

Personal Skills

_____ Considering other people's feelings
_____ Being able to get along well with others
_____ Accepting responsibility for my actions
_____ Respecting those in authority
_____ Taking care of my belongings
_____ Following school rules

My overall effort has been   3   2   1

Please explain anything you feel the teacher may need to know about yourself or your work.

_____

_____

_____

Please explain your feelings about my teaching.

_____

_____

_____

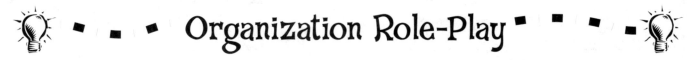

Organization Role-Play

As students get older and gain more and more responsibility, they will need to learn strategies toward strong organizational skills. Role-playing is an effective strategy to help students remember a new skill.

Begin the lesson with students in pairs. They should then brainstorm steps and/or strategies they do in order to remember their homework. They can include things they do to get their homework finished on time each day. Some possible answers students may give include the following:

- check the assignment book
- do homework immediately when they arrive at home
- keep the backpack by the door
- put finished homework in the backpack as soon as it is complete

After brainstorming, students share their ideas as the teacher writes them down on the chalkboard, overhead projector, or poster paper.

To implement the role-play, put students into groups of three. Pass out the role-play situation cards provided on page 73. Give one card to each group. This card will guide them through their practice time. Once practiced, students will present the play to the whole class.

After presenting, the class should decide which type of role-play was displayed. Was the situation a student who was organized or unorganized? Also, review strategies demonstrated in the role-play. Some questions to ask include the following:

What did you notice the student doing . . .

- when the teacher was reviewing the day's homework?
- when homework was completed at home?
- when he came home from school?

How do you think the student felt . . .

- when arriving at school?
- when talking to the teacher?

✓ **Tips:** Record the students' ideas and strategies in the role-plays on large poster paper and hang it in the room for further reference.

Have more role-play examples of an organized student than an unorganized student to better reinforce those skills.

Role-Play Situation Cards

Characters: Parent, Teacher, Student

Situation: I never have any late assignments!

Demonstrate to the class what an organized student looks and acts like. How does an organized student remember his or her homework? What steps does he or she take in order to remember and complete homework?

Start your role-play, pretending it is from the end of our school day and continue on through to the next morning until the beginning of the school day. Skip unimportant details, such as eating, dressing, etc.

Include in your role-play what the parent and teacher act like towards this well-organized student.

Use props to help the audience understand the goal.

Time: Keep the role-play short and to the point (five minutes at the maximum).

- -

Characters: Parent, Teacher, Student

Situation: How did I forget my homework again?

Demonstrate to the class what an unorganized student looks and acts like. How does an unorganized student not remember his or her homework? What steps does he or she not take in order to remember and complete homework?

Start your role-play, pretending it is from the end of the school day and continue on through to the next morning until the beginning of the school day. Skip unimportant details, such as eating, dressing, etc.

Include in your role-play what the parent and teacher act like towards this unorganized student.

Use props to help the audience understand the goal.

Time: Keep the role-play short and to the point (five minutes at the maximum).

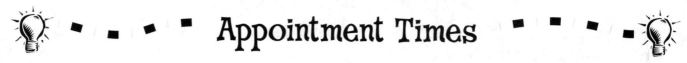

Appointment Times

Tired of asking students to pick a partner, and it resulting in hurt feelings or taking too much class time? A simple, efficient way to do this is to have the partner picked ahead of time, and not by the teacher.

It is important to do this activity at the beginning of the school year. The beginning of the year works best, because friendships or unfavorable opinions have not been formed. The students will all be on the same equal level.

Using the appointment book sheet on page 75, students fill in the book with names of people to be partners with. Ten or 12 slots is a good amount. The boys must get four or five girls' names, and the girls must get four or five boys' names on their appointment book. Students can say "no" to another student only if that person is already on their sheet or if the student is left needing only those of the opposite gender.

Students go around the room and find a person to sign up at the one o'clock time. Once the student finds a person with the one o'clock time open, they switch papers and each sign his or her name on the one o'clock time. Now, that time is filled and no one else can put his or her name on that time slot. Students continue the same procedure until all the times are filled in.

The students must find different people. No student can sign another's paper more than once. Also, it is extremely important that students remember to sign each other's paper and that they both sign for the same appointment time.

(*Note:* The appointment time has nothing to do with the actual time of day but is simply a creative way to get 12 partners. When a partner is needed, simply call out a random appointment time or have a student randomly pick a number one through twelve. Students will look at their appointment book sheet and go with the person whose name appears next to the corresponding time chosen. It is helpful to have those students stand up whose partner is not there that day. Then the teacher can then regroup those students for that activity.)

✓ **Tip:** Sometimes having all the students wandering around at once trying to fill in their appointments can be too confusing and leaves the less assertive students with no appointments. Another alternative is to have specified groups go at specified times. For example, have all the boys stand and find a girl for the one o'clock time. Next, for the two o'clock time, have all the girls stand and find a boy. For the three o'clock time, have the left side of the class stand and find someone sitting on the right side and so on.

Appointment Books

APPOINTMENTS

12:00 _____

1:00 _____

2:00 _____

3:00 _____

4:00 _____

5:00 _____

APPOINTMENTS

_____ 6:00

_____ 7:00

_____ 8:00

_____ 9:00

_____ 10:00

_____ 11:00

APPOINTMENTS

12:00 _____

1:00 _____

2:00 _____

3:00 _____

4:00 _____

5:00 _____

APPOINTMENTS

_____ 6:00

_____ 7:00

_____ 8:00

_____ 9:00

_____ 10:00

_____ 11:00

Sticks, Numbers, and Bins

Some quick and easy ideas to manage your classroom are sticks, student numbers, and special boxes for homework.

Sticks

The sticks are large, craft sticks (tongue depressors). The first day of school give each student one stick. On the stick is the student's name in black permanent marker. The student's job is to decorate it anyway he or she wishes—color both sides or one side, use markers or crayons, etc. Once complete, the stick is held in a specially designated cup where it remains all year. These sticks are used for everything. Whenever you need a volunteer, pick a stick. To raffle off an extra item or poster, pick a stick. To get a quick partner, pick a stick. To pick a special helper for a special task, pick a stick.

Student Numbers

The numbers are given to the students for organizational purposes. However, they come in handy for other circumstances, too. In most grade books, the students' names are in alphabetical order. Next to each name is a number 1–30. Obviously, the first student in alphabetical order will be number one, and so on. At the start of the year, put the numbers on the corner of each desk using black self-adhesive numbers found at any office supply store. Those same numbers are put on the student's homework bin, any class textbook, and on any other student material to be used throughout the year.

Why are numbers helpful? It really keeps the anonymity of the student and allows you to reuse items from year to year, because there are no names on books, math manipulatives, and other classroom items. Things turned in using number order are already alphabetized for your grade book, and the teacher can use the numbers for other random events, such as having all the odd numbers line up or all the two-digit numbers get the mail.

During the first week of school, tell the students they each have a number and that it is their number all year long for everything. For example, a student named Kate Calm would be number four. Her desk will have a four on it, and so will her homework bin, math tool kit, social studies book, science book, and reading novels. Any item labeled with a four would belong to Kate Calm.

Homework Bins

Homework bins are another organizational tool. Each bin is marked with a student number (this allows repeated use from year to year). Each morning the students turn in the night's homework in their bin. This works great because the teacher can collect the work in alphabetical order for grading and recording purposes. If there is no name on a paper, the papers are alphabetical so the teacher can easily find the owner. The homework bins also make it very easy to see who has not turned in his or her homework, because the bin will be empty. The teacher can talk to that student immediately. It possibly might be that he or she just forgot to turn in the homework. Now, the teacher will no longer have a pile of random papers and can quickly tell whose work is missing.

✔ **Tip:** Have a teacher mailbox on the desk for students to turn in any permission slips, notes from parents, or other forms. Keep the homework bins for student work only.

Homework Families

It is a good idea to have a permanent group or family to which each student belongs for the entire school year. The possibilities are endless on what the teacher can use them for. Families should be no larger than four people. For students younger than third grade, three people is the limit. Possible uses include the following:

- Families can meet in the morning to get ready for the day. The teacher can have a list of criteria on the board to meet before the day starts, and each group member gets each other ready. For example, the criteria list can be the following: turn in math homework, turn in permission slip, push in chair, get pencil ready. Once the group has completed the tasks, the teacher can briefly meet with the families and find out immediately who's missing certain items, etc.

- Families can meet at the end of the day to get ready to go home. Members can check each other's assignment books and backpacks for all the needed materials for homework.

- Homework families are a quick way to get groups ready for any specific activity.

- Families can meet to work on higher-level brain teasers or word problems before the day starts or do problems from the previous day's math lessons.

- They can function as study groups for any test or quiz.

- Families can also read together.

Once they are placed in their family, have them come up with a name, handshake, and slogan or song. This will help increase family bonding.

> ✓ **Tips:** Wait about three weeks before placing students into these families. Because these groups are together all year, the teacher should observe so as to choose the best possible combinations that will help facilitate cooperative learning. Emphasize that this grouping is like a family. Tell them that, like your real family, the student cannot get rid of his or her sister or brother if they are annoying. The student must learn to work it out.
>
> Homework families are only one type of group. Students should be placed with other students as often as possible. Do not limit all cooperative learning to these homework families.

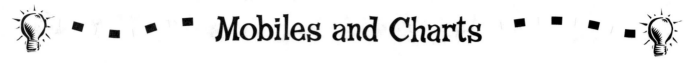

Mobiles and Charts

"What Should I Do Now?" Mobile

Teachers often hear that famous question "What should I do now?" from students. It may bother some teachers who go through agonizing efforts to make centers, enrichment activities, games, etc., interesting. The students still do not know what to do when they rush through the assignment.

This mobile is a simple way to let the students know exactly what to do without having to come to the teacher. It frees teachers up to help those who need it, and, most importantly, it gives the students a sense of independence.

At the top of the mobile, write the question, "What should I do now?" Hang below it all the different activities in which the teacher would like them to participate. The teacher can hang it from the ceiling and write an activity on both sides so it can be viewed from any perspective. Or, hang it against a wall and turn over only those activities the teacher feels are most appropriate for that time of day. For example, the teacher may only want the computer game option showing when the computer is free.

> ✓ **Tip:** Before hanging the mobile, explain to the class each activity option, where to find it, and how many can be participating at once.

Help! I Can't Find It!

It never seems to fail. The day an assignment is due, there is that one student who cannot find his or her assignment. Inevitably, the child will seek the teacher out for help. To avoid class interruptions and having to take time to help the child locate the missing paper, try the following idea.

Have a list of steps to go through posted in the room, as well as in every child's folder. (See page 79.) This puts the responsibility back onto the student. Steps should be listed in the order of the most likely place to the least likely place. Steps can include the following:

- Check their homework bin. (It is possible that the student already turned it in.)

- Check their personal mailbox, folder, backpack, and textbook.

- If it is not in any of the places listed above, he or she should go into the "extra copies" basket and get a new sheet to start over.

> ✓ **Tip:** It is always a good idea to make five extra copies of work and keep them in an "extra copies" basket. Make the basket accessible to the students.

"Help! I Can't Find It!"

1. Look in **ALL FOLDERS,** especially my home folder and the folder of the missing subject.

2. Look in my **HOMEWORK BIN.** Check the bin above and below mine.

3. Look inside my **BOOK** of the missing subject.

   Example: My social studies study guide is missing. I will look in my social studies book.

4. Look inside my **BACKPACK**.

5. Look inside my **DESK.** If my desk is very messy, I will empty it and go through the loose papers.

6. If I still have not found it after checking everywhere, I will go to the **EXTRA COPIES** bin and do it over at recess or free time.

Bulletin Boards

Use a colored background paper that can stay up all year, or, if possible, use fabric because it lasts longer.

Make the bulletin board interactive rather than decorative. If used in this way, students will pay attention to it. Otherwise, they will look at the cute decor once and overlook it the rest of the month. An interactive board can have review questions, word scrambles, matching definitions to important vocabulary, math questions, geography questions, etc. The teacher can change the questions monthly and offer extra credit for them. Meanwhile, the rest of the board can remain relatively the same.

To decrease the amount of grading, teachers can have a spiral notebook with the answers listed for the students to use or let a student or parent helper grade the answers.

Geo-Genius

Design a geography bulletin board with maps, states and capital flash cards, world puzzles, a globe, atlas, etc. Each week pose at least three geography questions. There are many resource books which have questions already made up. Laminate the questions and put them up on the board. The teacher can then change them easily and save them for years to come. On Friday, the answers are due. The students turn them into a special Geo-Genius bucket. Have a student or parent helper grade them, and announce the winners at the end of the day. The prize can be whatever the teacher decides.

✓ **Tips:** Allow partners to work together on the questions. Children tend to need the reinforcement at first.

Design a special form for their answers. (See page 81 for a sample.) This helps for grading purposes when all the answers are organized in the same manner.

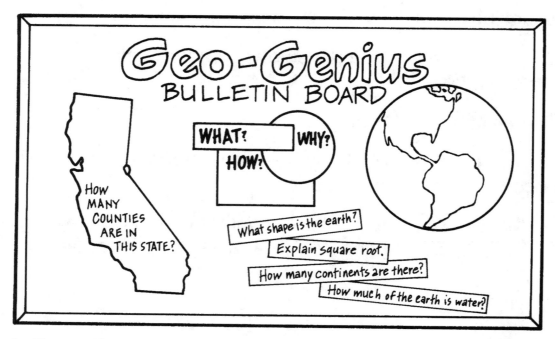

Geo-Genius

Name: _____ Date: _____

1(A) _____

1(B) _____

2(A) _____

2(B) _____

3(A) _____

3(B) _____

 # A Clear Contract

This contract activity will clearly define everyone's job and help establish clear expectations.

1. To reinforce the contract idea, begin the activity with a discussion of what a contract is and when it is used.

2. Have students look up the word "contract" in the dictionary. To help emphasize its importance, discuss how it is a legal, binding document.

3. Divide the chalkboard in half. On one side, at the top, write "Students." On the other side, write "Teacher."

4. The students then have a brainstorming session in small groups to answer the following question: "What responsibilities do the students have in order to have a successful, smooth-running classroom?"

5. Students write down their ideas. When finished, each group shares them with the whole class as the teacher records the answers on the board under "Students."

6. Then do the same activity, but this time focusing on the teacher's role and/or responsibilities. Some sample ideas are as follows:

Students	Teacher
listen	listen
put items away	help students with work
wait their turn	grade papers fairly
not tease others	give praise
follow directions	learn everyone's name
keep desks clean	explain things in a fun, interesting way

7. As a whole class, try to narrow the list down and combine common items. The teacher may want the students to feel ownership and be willing to agree and abide by the contract. If an item seems to cause great disagreement or concern, try rewording or omitting it altogether. The teacher may add some of his or her own ideas to both lists. Some of the ideas can be non-negotiable, such as "Students will respect school property and each other's property."

8. Once the lists are complete, make a large poster of the contract to keep in the room as a reminder.

9. Have each student and the teacher sign it. In addition, make 8½" x 11" copies for students to sign and keep in a special folder. (See page 83 for a sample.)

Student/Teacher Contract

The Students will . . .   The Teacher will . . .

Student Signature: _____ Date: _____

Teacher Signature: _____ Date: _____

 Acronyms

Journals

After students write in their journals about any particular topic, they can switch journals with a partner and respond. However, often students do not know how to respond. The acronym below works great for journal response writing. This acronym will help them focus their writing and get them started.

N = Name (simply means to address the person to whom the student is writing)

A = Acknowledge (means to react to what the writer has said)

A = Ask (means to ask something about which the student is curious that has not been mentioned or to ask something to get the writer thinking)

G = Give your opinion (means to tell the writer what you think about the topic)

S = Sign your name

An example of a response might be the following:

> Sam,
>
> Your thoughts about Fudge being spoiled are really great. You seem to really relate to Fudge's brother. You probably have a younger brother who drives you nuts, too. How do you think Charlie should have handled the situation?
>
> I think Charlie needs to ignore Fudge's actions. It is only going to drive him crazy if he doesn't. I don't think his mom helps enough either.
>
> Sue

End of the Day

Acronyms can also help in other areas. For example, the acronyms below help students to remember their "stuff" at the end of the day. Of course, the teacher can create one that works well for his or her students. The idea of an acronym is to help students remember what is needed to go home. It is an easy tool to incorporate into the end routine.

M = Mail
A = Assignment book
T = Texts
H = Homework

or

H = Homework
A = Assignment book
M = Mail

PACK

Have students become part of the PACK (Projects Aimed at Challenging Kids). Design a center in the room where students can go and work on numerous projects in all subjects. When they complete a certain number of projects, they can become PACK kids. They should receive a special certificate for this accomplishment. Or, enlarge a picture of a cute animal for each student and add stickers to it. Once the student has received five stickers for completing five PACK activities, he or she can receive a reward of some type. To save time, find various enrichment ideas for the PACK center in several teacher resource books on the market.

Learning Ideas

If stars dropped out of heaven,
And if flowers took their place,
The sky would still look very fair,
And fair earth's face.

Winged angels might fly down to us
To pluck the stars,
But we could only long for flowers
Beyond the cloudy bars.

If I were a Queen,
What would I do?
I'd make you King,
And I'd wait on you.

If I were a King,
What would I do?
I'd make you Queen,
For I'd marry you.

THE BOW WOW PALS

MICHIGAN

There's No "I" In Team!

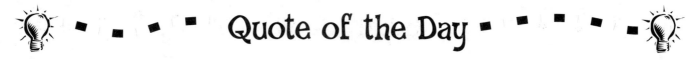

Quote of the Day

Start each day with some higher-level thoughts. Quotes are clever, interesting ways to reinforce morals and values. Pick a student each day to read a quote of the day, or make it a class job to write it on the board. He or she should stand in front of the class and read it two or three times aloud. Next, let the class informally pair up and discuss the meaning of the quote. The teacher may have to do a few lessons on reading literally and figuratively. Amelia Bedelia books are great examples of this. After the lesson, the students will understand. The teacher can also hang the quote in the room for student reference.

A great quote to start off the school year is, "Every new beginning is some other beginning's end." Some other favorite quotes to use include the following:

- People may doubt what you say, but they will always believe what you do.
- You miss 100% of the shots you never take.
- Success comes before work only in the dictionary.
- The more you know, the more you know you don't know.
- You may delay, but time will not.
- A friend stands behind you when all others leave.
- Nothing is permanent but change.

✓ **Tips:** Write the quote on sentence strips. Laminate and hang the quote on a sentence strip holder. Hang the holder in the room and change the quotes as it fills up.

To take the activity one step further, ask the class to give an example of when this quote could be useful in their lives.

> "Every new beginning is some other beginning's end."

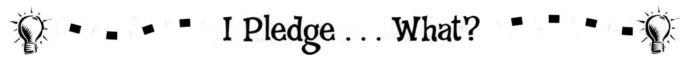

I Pledge . . . What?

Many teachers have their class stand each morning and recite the Pledge of Allegiance. It can become so rote to students that it is almost meaningless. Here is a simple activity to help peak their interest and give the pledge some meaning.

1. Put the phrases of the pledge on individual sentence strips and laminate. One way to break the pledge up into several parts is as follows:

> I pledge allegiance

> to the flag of the United States of America

> and to the Republic for which it stands,

> one Nation under God,

> indivisible, with liberty

> and justice for all.

2. Make six or seven sets to allow for a small group activity.

3. Put students in small groups and give each group a set of sentence strips facing down. Make sure the sentence strips are mixed up when handed to each group.

4. Instruct the students not to touch the strips. Do not tell them what is written on the strips.

5. On the count of three, they are to take the strips and put them in order as fast as possible.

6. Once they flip them over, they will quickly recognize the words. When the activity is finished, the group should stand.

7. After every group has successfully organized their strips, assign each group one phrase to define in their own words.

8. Once each group can define the meaning of their team's phrase, one representative from each group goes to the front of the room.

9. He or she should stand in the correct order of the pledge holding the strip in front of himself or herself.

10. One at a time, the team representatives read their phrase. Each then asks for three volunteers to guess the meaning of the phrase.

11. He or she then tells the answer the team discussed.

Challenge Club

For students who seem to be such great spellers that they test beyond the traditional spelling book and weekly tests, have them be a part of the Challenge Club. Anyone with 100% on the pretest will be in the club for that week. Those students who excel in spelling will be in it every week!

The Challenge Club students pick ten words they do not know how to spell from their own creative stories, dictionary, and/or reading novel. Once they pick their ten words, they will have several activities to do with those words. (See page 89 for a sample.) Activities include the following:

- Write a brief definition of each word.

- Make a word find.

- Make a word scramble.

- Put the words in ABC order.

- Form a picture out of the words.

- Draw a picture of each of the words.

- Rewrite the words using cursive writing.

- Write a sentence for each word using alliteration.

- Write each word as fancily and decoratively as possible.

- Write a postcard to a friend using five or more words from the list.

- Create a cartoon strip using five or more of the words.

- Divide each word into syllables.

The ideas are endless. The point is to do activities that are fun and help the child remember how to spell the words. Students pick the words so they have ownership of their spelling, and the teacher accommodates for all the different ability levels.

Challenge Club also works well with the nontraditional spelling programs. If the teacher has a program where students build their own lists, then use the activities for practice.

✓ **Tip:** Keep the amount of words small. Ten is a good amount, because the words have no pattern to aid in memorizing and the students will not get bogged down building their list. Preview the list to make sure the words are appropriate and useful, and also check their pronunciation of the words.

Challenge Club Form

This week you are in the Challenge Club. To complete your assignment for the week, there are several activities you must do.

1. On the spaces provided below, write your final list of spelling words in alphabetical order.

2. Across from each word, write a short definition, using a dictionary. You must be able to understand the definition, and the definition you choose must clearly explain the meaning of the word. For example, if the word is "honesty," the definition cannot be, "to be honest."

Word List	Definitions
1. _____	_____
2. _____	_____
3. _____	_____
4. _____	_____
5. _____	_____
6. _____	_____
7. _____	_____
8. _____	_____
9. _____	_____
10. _____	_____

3. Divide every word into syllables. Use a dictionary if you are unsure. For example, the word "pupil" would be divided into two syllables: pu-pil. Next to each word that has three or more syllables, draw a happy face. The happy face tells you that this is a tough word.

4. Using the first five words on your list, write one sentence using alliteration for each word. For example, "The <u>pupil</u> picked petals from the purple petunia." Underline the spelling word in the sentence.

Join the Class Work Force

Job Application

Many teachers have class jobs. Instead of assigning jobs or randomly choosing jobs, consider having the students actually apply for their job. After explaining each job, pass out a paper that has each job title and an explanation of the requirements and responsibilities. For example, if the job is a messenger, the description would be, "Someone the teacher calls upon to deliver various materials and/or information to another adult at the school. The requirements of this job would be as follows: trustworthy, quick walker, reliable, knows the school layout, and knows the teachers." Part of the application process is to fill out the application carefully, accurately, and thoroughly. Along with having experience or meeting the requirements, the student also must fill out the application correctly. (See page 91.)

 Tip: Have students apply only the first time jobs are presented in the year. Doing so every time jobs change would be too tedious. Do, however, keep a record of who applied for each job. This way, when jobs are assigned in the future you can give specific jobs to those who applied for them. Allow for additional applications during the year.

Class Patrol

One job to have included on your job board is a class patrol. This is a job for two people in your class. The patrol's main responsibility is to maintain the class rules when the teacher is not in the classroom. Sometimes situations arise when the teacher needs to step out for a minute. Or, if the class has an inside lunch recess, it is nice to have someone else watching the class and maintaining order other than the recess supervisor. The patrol is in charge of watching the class to make sure everyone is following the class rules, behaving in a good manner, and acting safely and respectfully. If a patrol person sees someone misbehaving, that child's name goes on the chalkboard, and the teacher will speak with him or her when the teacher returns into the classroom. The patrol does not issue consequences.

It is wise to have a list of expectations written for the patrol to use as guidelines—what the teacher feels warrants a child's name being written on the board. Do not leave this up to the patrol's discretion. Often, it is too tempting to get someone into trouble or to not tell on a buddy.

Change the patrol job every week or two. When the teacher leaves the room, make sure to announce to the room that the patrol is now on duty. The patrol job is a voluntary position and should be only for those who are responsible and really want it.

✓ Tip: Decide on the guidelines together as a class. This way everyone is aware of what is expected and what the patrol is expected to do.

Job Application Form

1. Print name.

_____   _____
          (last)   (first)

2. Write the name of the job for which you are applying below.

_____

_____

3. Print your grade level, age, and date.

_____   _____   _____
 (grade level)   (age)   (date)

4. Do you have any experience with this job?   Yes   No

   If yes, please explain your experience.

_____

_____

_____

_____

_____

5. Using complete sentences, explain why you should be chosen for this job.

_____

_____

_____

6. List two strengths you have that would help you perform this job.

_____

_____

_____
   (Student Signature)

 # Curiosity Questions

Oftentimes, there is not a lot of room or time for exploration into other areas in which the students may be interested. Teachers often say students need to take ownership of their learning, yet rarely are they given the opportunity to decide what they learn. Simply by being flexible in the scheduling, on occasion, the teacher can have a class vote on which subject the teacher should start next—math or social studies. This is not always feasible, but when it is possible, why not let them decide? It means a great deal to them.

One way to incorporate student-directed learning is through curiosity questions. This is when the teacher has the students write down a question they have about basic occurrences in life. Things they have often wondered about like the following: Why do we sneeze? What is an itch? Why is the sky blue?

Students can write down on a slip of paper the following information: the date of the question, the question itself, and their name. (See sample below.) At the bottom of the slip is a line for the due date. This then gets stapled to the top of the notebook paper of the child who has the researched answer.

How the research works is up to the teacher. The teacher can assign each child a week to research their question and answer, or have everyone researching questions at the same time with the same due date. The teacher can have questions researched with partners or in groups. Another possibility is to have individual students create a poster about their question or use a software program to create a mini slide show. Five slides work well for this activity. Or, the teacher can let the class decide. Since the students thought of the questions, they will take interest in how to present the findings. The research should not take much time, since the questions are very specific. Students should be able to research their question in one week.

✓ **Tip:** Hang all the curiosity questions and a brief explanation on a bulletin board. By displaying them, all students can look at each other's responses. The teacher can have a saying at the top of the bulletin board, such as "Curiosity Did Not Kill the Cat . . . This Time!"

Curiosity Question

By _____

My question is _____

_____

Date submitted: _____   Due date: _____

The Word of the Week

A fun way to add extra vocabulary to your students learning, and eventually their writing, is to have a Word of the Week. Find a special spot on a bulletin board or chalkboard. Hang a creative sign announcing "The Word of the Week." Under the sign, pick a word that is useful and teaches something at the same time. Words such as *punctual, enthusiasm, independent, compassionate,* and *sympathy* are words the students can use.

How does it work? Under the sign and the word, have an envelope with copies of the study sheet shown below. The students are responsible for learning the spelling, meaning, and part of speech for each week's word. The definition can be simple but should be from a dictionary. This activity is great for promoting the use of dictionary skills.

Make the Word of the Week worth an additional five points on their final spelling test. The word spelled correctly is two points, the correct definition is two points, and the correct part of speech is worth one point. This can be extra credit points or part of their final spelling score.

✓ **Tips:** Hang the word up on Monday and pronounce it for the entire class. Have students repeat the pronunciation. Students do the Word of the Week on Friday's spelling test from memory. Have a special spot on your spelling test form to fill in the definition, circle the part of speech, and write the word. If students take their spelling test on notebook paper, it is best to have a Word of the Week form to insure accuracy and consistency in their answers.

- -

Word of the Week

Word: _____

Part of Speech: Noun   Verb   Adjective

Definition: _____

_____

_____

_____

_____

Poem of the Month

To introduce poems, present a poem or two each month. Pick a theme for that month and find poems to fit it. For example, the October poems could be about Halloween. December poems could be about winter. February poems could focus on friendships. Find poems that are kid friendly and have interesting rhythm.

Copy a class set of the poems, three-hole punch them, and pass them out at the beginning of each month. First, read the poem aloud modeling the rhythm and correct pronunciation for the students. Then have the students read it. Splitting up the task into smaller parts keeps their attention longer, and keeps the whole class involved. For example, the girls can stand and read the first two stanzas, then the boys can stand to read the next two, and continue to alternate. There are a variety of ways to alternate the readings. Depending on the poem, the teacher may read it more than once using different groups.

Once it has been read, discuss the rhythm, the special wording, the description used, etc. However, there is no need to go into great detail (e.g., iambic pentameter). Exposure to different types of reading is knowledge itself. Remember to get poems that do not rhyme, too.

An extension activity is to have students create a poem using similar characteristics. If the poem verses are in couplets, have them write couplet poems. If the poem uses spelling in a creative way to emphasize the poem's meaning, the students do the same.

Another suggestion is to enlarge each poem to poster size, if there is access to this type of machine. Have a volunteer color and/or decorate them to be hung in the hallway outside the classroom door. Each month the poem is taken down and given away to two students chosen randomly by using the name sticks (page 76). Replace these with new ones for the next month. Once the student receives the poster-size poem, it is his or her job to read it aloud to the class one last time.

> ✓ **Tip:** Three-hole punch the poems and have the students put them all in a binder or folder specified for poems. They should save them each month, and by June they will have a fun collection. If there are no extra folders for this, consider using the students' reading folders.

Cooperation Totem Pole

Working together in a classroom environment is very common. However, it can also be challenging for students to do this effectively. A fun way to do some team building is to make a totem pole that accurately reflects the team. This activity also ties in nicely with Native American units.

A group of four students sit together and decide what they all have in common. Perhaps they all go to camp over the summer, they all like to ski, they all have a dog for a pet, or they all play an instrument. Whatever they come up with will be the foundation for their team name. So if they all have a dog for a pet, they can call themselves "The Dog Gone Kids" or "The Bow Wow Pals." After they have a group name, one person makes a sign with the group name written on it in a creative way.

Next, each member picks one family tradition he or she celebrates—maybe family visits to Michigan to go boating every summer. Another student might have a special song his or her family sings. Once each student decides on a family tradition, he or she then creates a symbol of it to put on the totem pole. For example, a boat or picture of the state of Michigan might be chosen by the student who goes boating in Michigan every summer.

In the end, the group will have five pieces: a sign with the group name and four individual symbols representing each member's family tradition. These symbols are then fastened to a totem pole structure. Build a pole by taking large butcher paper, rolling it into a pole shape, and taping it closed. Fasten the symbols on to cover the tape. At the top of the pole, place the group's sign.

Once the pole is assembled, a short paragraph explaining each symbol should be written and fastened to the back of the totem pole. Each group will then present their totem pole to the rest of the class.

✔ **Tip:** Symbols should be created from construction paper and not be a drawing. They are visually more appealing and are more representative of an actual totem pole.

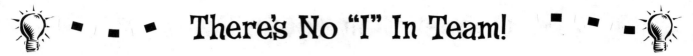

There's No "I" In Team!

A clever way to introduce cooperative procedures in your classroom is to do a cooperation activity during the first week of school. Follow the instructions below.

1. Buy five precut puzzles.

2. On each puzzle, write one word from the phrase "There's No 'I' In Team!" or any other phrase.

3. Break each puzzle up one at a time and put in a baggy.

4. Divide the class into five groups and give each group a baggy. Do not tell them what the puzzle says or any other information. The mystery keeps it exciting.

5. Once complete, students bring their completed puzzle to a table and then the class rearranges all five completed puzzles to make a complete phrase.

6. Once the entire phrase is complete, have a class discussion on what the quote means and how they can enforce it throughout the year. This is a good time to develop cooperative group procedures to follow.

7. Have some students glue the puzzles on a poster board and then have each student sign the board declaring his commitment to the phrase.

✓ **Tip:** Instead of buying puzzles, create your own. Write one word on a piece of poster board. Sketch out puzzle pieces on the back. Cut out the puzzle, and it is ready.